Portals to Freedom

HOWARD COLBY IVES

Bahá'í
PUBLISHING
Wilmette, Illinois

Bahá'í Publishing
415 Linden Avenue, Wilmette, Illinois 60091-2844

15 14 13 12   4 3 2 1

Library of Congress Cataloging-in-Publication Data
Ives, Howard Colby.
  Portals to freedom / by Howard Colby Ives.
     p. cm.
  Includes bibliographical references (p. 215).
  ISBN 978-1-931847-99-5 (alk. paper)
  1. 'Abdu'l-Bahá, 1844–1921. 2. Bahais—Biography. 3. Bahai Faith. 4. Ives,
Howard Colby. 5. Spiritual biography. I. Title.
  BP393.I8 2012
  297.9'3092—dc23
  [B]
                                        2012001997

Cover design by Andrew Johnson
Book design by Patrick Falso
Photograph of 'Abdu'l-Bahá taken in Dublin, NH reproduced with permission of the
Bahá'í International Community

To
Shoghi Effendi
The Grandson of
'Abdu'l-Bahá

By Him Appointed
Guardian of the Bahá'í Faith

CONTENTS

CONTENTS

CONTENTS

'Abdu'l-Bahá in Dublin, NH

PREFACE TO THE 2012 EDITION

In preparing this new edition of *Portals to Freedom,* a work previously published in the UK, the editors have adjusted various spellings and punctuation marks in order to conform with modern American usage, and in order to make the book more easily read by the modern reader. The publisher has been careful, however, not to alter the content in such a way that the original intent of the author is in any way compromised. It should be noted that the views and understandings presented by the author regarding the Bahá'í Faith should not be considered authoritative, but should be seen as representing the author's personal understandings.

Portals to Freedom was written at a time when many of the current translations of the writings of the central figures of the Bahá'í Faith had not yet been published. Throughout the volume, author Howard Colby Ives refers to passages, the wording of which no longer matches the current editions of the works being cited. Many of the early translations, which were circulated at the time of the author's writing, have since been replaced with newer translations and are no longer in print. Where possible, passages have been replaced with up-to-date translations, or endnotes have been inserted to refer to current editions of the works referenced. Some of the works cited—*Tablets of 'Abdu'l-Bahá Abbas, vols. 1–3; Bahá'í Scriptures;* and *Bahá'í World Faith*—contain passages of which there are questions concerning accuracy of translation and authenticity of original documents. These works are cited here, however, in an effort to accurately preserve the book that Mr. Ives wrote and to reflect the material that was available to him at the time of his writing. There are also some instances in which words are attributed to 'Abdu'l-Bahá for which no sources have been found. It is possible in some cases that Mr. Ives was recounting words spoken by 'Abdu'l-Bahá in his presence, which were not otherwise formally recorded.

It should be noted that throughout the volume, Mr. Ives refers to the reported utterances of 'Abdu'l-Bahá. These utterances should not be considered authoritative statements of Bahá'í teachings nor should they be considered Bahá'í scripture. 'Abdu'l-Bahá, as the son and appointed successor of Bahá'u'lláh—the Prophet and Founder of the Bahá'í Faith—is, from a Bahá'í perspective, the authorized interpreter of the writings of his Father as well as the perfect exemplar of the Faith's teachings. The writings of 'Abdu'l-Bahá are considered divine in origin and authoritative in nature. His recorded utterances, however, do not have the same status as they are less reliable renderings of His words.

Portals to Freedom

INTRODUCTION

I beg of Thee, O my God, by Thy most exalted Word which Thou hast ordained as the Divine Elixir unto all who are in Thy realm, the Elixir through whose potency the crude metal of human life hath been transmuted into purest gold, O Thou in Whose hands are both the visible and invisible kingdoms, to ordain that my choice be conformed to Thy choice and my wish to Thy wish, that I may be entirely content with that which Thou didst desire, and be wholly satisfied with what Thou didst destine for me by Thy bounteousness and favor.
—Bahá'u'lláh, *Prayers and Meditations,* p. 53

What is that mystery underlying human life that gives to events and to persons the power of mutation, of transformation? If one had never before seen a seed, nor heard of its latent life, how difficult to believe that only the cold earth, the warm sun, the descending showers, and the gardener's care were needed to cause its miraculous transformation into the growing form, the budding beauty, the intoxicating fragrance of the rose!

Or who can understand the reason why a chance perusal of a book, the presence of a friend, or the meeting with a stranger often alters a determined course of action, profoundly affects our attitude toward life, and, not seldom, so nearly reaches the roots of being and the springs of action that never after is life quite the same?

It is as if some super-Luther Burbank had, by that seemingly chance event, grafted into the branch of our crabapple being the bud of the Tree of Knowledge, or into the bramble of the wilderness of human thought the rose of paradise.

To this mystery of mysteries the philosophy of the schoolmen offers no adequate explanation. We only know that it is a common experience of us all. The effort toward the description of this catalysis is the essence of all poetry; the abortive attempt to explain it is at the root of all philosophy, while the experience of it is the one cause underlying the transformation of human life and character. All history is its witness and every saint its justification.

In offering to the reader this inadequate account of one such experience, my only excuse is its totality, its all-inclusiveness, its grandeur. It is unique not because it is rare, since every contact of man with his fellowmen demonstrates it, but because of its supremacy over other transforming contacts. One might liken it to the difference in effect between touching a cold clod and the grasping of a galvanic battery, or the meeting with a debased criminal and the meeting with an Abraham Lincoln.

To those who met 'Abdu'l-Bahá in the summer of 1912, when He spent eight months in this country, such comparisons will seem highly inadequate. While to many that meeting did not convey more than a contact with personified dignity, beauty, wisdom, and selflessness, and so led them, at least, to higher altitudes of thought and life, to hundreds of others that meeting was the door to undreamed-of worlds; to a new, a boundless, an eternal life.

We realize the difficulties faced in attempting to bring to the reader a quarter of a century later, the atmosphere created by this meeting for those who had the eyes to see, the ears to hear, and minds to comprehend, even slightly, the new and divine world opened before the eager and courageous feet. In fact to do so with any degree of accurate completeness is all but impossible. To those bred in the Christian tradition one might ask what would be the probable effect upon them if they could have been among the audience when the Sermon on the Mount was spoken, or if one of them, like John, could have reclined upon the breast of the Master. Without daring to suggest that the comparison is parallel, my own experience, when brought into close association with 'Abdu'l-Bahá, was so overwhelming, so fraught with sensations suggesting an entrance into a new and super-mundane world, that I can think of no other comparison more adequate.

I do not propose in relating these experiences to minimize my own reaction to this great experience by presenting it with even the slightest suggestion of materialistic or pseudoscientific explanations. It is my work to report as faithfully as possible what I saw and heard and experienced during these meetings and conversations. If at times the recounting flavors of a fancy bordering on the fantastic, I may comfort myself with reflection on the possible terms applied to Peter, James, and John the fishermen, when they attempted to describe to their fellow-laborers the effect that the Master's presence had upon them. What epithets must the former lovers and associates of Mary Magdalene have applied to her!

To me, a man of middle age, a Unitarian Clergyman, a student since youth of religions and philosophies, the experience had a disturbing quality somewhat cataclysmic. Why should this man be able so to upset all my preconceived notions and conceptions of values by His mere presence? Was it that He seemed to exude from His very being an atmosphere of love and understanding such as I had never dreamed? Was it the resonant voice, modulated to a music which caught the heart? Was it the aura of happiness, touched at times with a sadness implying the bearing of the burden of all the sin and sorrow of the world, which always surrounded Him? Was it the commingled majesty and humility of His every gesture and word, which was perhaps His most obvious characteristic? How can one answer such questions? Those who saw and heard 'Abdu'l-Bahá during those memorable months will share with me the sense of the inadequacy of words to communicate the incommunicable.

At the time I met 'Abdu'l-Bahá, in the spring of 1912, He was sixty-eight years of age. Of these, twelve years had been spent in exile with His spiritual as well as physical Father, Bahá'u'lláh, in Baghdád, Constantinople, and Adrianople. Then forty years, to a day, in the Turkish prison-fortress of 'Akká, ten miles from Mt. Carmel, on the coast of Palestine. Because of their staunch adherence to their faith in Bahá'u'lláh as the Manifestation of God, 'Abdu'l-Bahá with about seventy others, had sacrificed all that they had, preferring imprisonment and inward freedom with Him to outward freedom and spiritual bondage without Him. With the overthrow of the tyrannous reign of 'Abdu'l-Hamid, by the Young Turk Party in 1908, this long exile and imprisonment ended and that voice and presence was free to prove to the world what He had so completely demonstrated, that the only prison is the prison of self.

To what marvelous inner life of the spirit could be ascribed, I asked myself, the fact that this man, born of a long line of Persian nobility; accustomed to every luxury until his eighth year; followed by a half-century of exile, torture, and prison-life, could emerge into the modern world of Paris, London, and New York and dominate every experience with a calm control of circumstance; a clarifying exposure of superficialities; a joyous love for all humanity, which never condemned but with forgiveness brought shame?

It is with the hope that, to a degree, the following pages may approach an answer to this question that they are offered to the reader.

CHAPTER ONE

RETROSPECT. SPIRITUAL BANKRUPTCY.
A DAWNING HOPE. THE GOLDEN SILENCE.

O friend, the heart is the dwelling of eternal mysteries, make it not the home of fleeting fancies; waste not the treasure of thy precious life in employment with this swiftly passing world. Thou comest from the world of holiness—bind not thine heart to the earth; thou art a dweller in the court of nearness—choose not the homeland of the dust.
—Bahá'u'lláh, *The Seven Valleys*, p. 34

My life divides itself, in retrospect, sharply in two. The years before I met 'Abdu'l-Bahá look to me now much as the ten-year-old child might be imagined to regard his matrix life, assuming him capable of that keen vision. The comparison is apt, also, from another angle; for, just as a child of ten has still before him experiences of vast and unimagined heights and depths, splendor and shadow, so I, the twenty-five year old youth of the spirit, look back, indeed, upon the forty-six years of gestation, recognizing the fact of that necessity if birth were to occur, but beyond that fact knowing little or nothing of the trivial causes that could lead to such effects. How much less, then, is it possible to estimate the future of the twice-born soul throughout unimaginable ages of life in all the worlds of God? If the wood in which the earthly sap flows briskly still is capable of such a flame, how great the conflagration when, freed from the laws of the world of nature, the fire kindled from the Sinaitic Tree becomes ablaze! Truly, birth of the body is a great event but, compared with the second birth, the first is only a feeble significance.

The fall and winter of 1911–12 is a period marked in my memory as months of great unhappiness. Life, in all that composed its deepest values, seemed to have left me high and dry on the banks of its swiftly flowing stream. Outwardly all was well but that inward voice that adds, "All is well indeed," was silent. I know of no greater disappointment, no more terrible depression than that which comes to the sincere soul who, seeking God, finds Him not.

For many years I had found myself unable to accept the conventional connotations of such words as *God, Faith, Heaven, Hell, Prayer, Christ, Eternal Life,* and others of so-called religious significance. In very early manhood I had come to grips with the goblins of superstition masquerading as churchly creeds and had cast them out, but no satisfying, spirit-lifting convictions had come to take their places. Perhaps for ten years my thought-life was frankly and positively agnostic. But these were great years nevertheless, for they were portals to freedom. But, alas, that freedom had failed to bring peace. I began to suspect that freedom without a guide and teacher fell little short of anarchy. True, I still had the teachings and life of Jesus of Nazareth, and never had I faded in love for them. But I failed woefully in the practice of them. And even a casual glance at the lives around me and the civilization men called "Christian," convinced me that so far as any practical parallel between words and deeds were concerned there were few, if any, Christians in the world, and certainly no expressions of social, economic, and national life worthy of such a name. Besides this objective fact, impossible to evade or deny, I was confronted by the even greater difficulty of the confused thought-life created by years of scientific, philosophical, and theological study and reading.

In all these crosscurrents of human speculation my frail skiff had all it could do to keep afloat, and the struggling oarsman little hope of finding his desired haven by following any one of them.

One day I found in the library of a village rector, where we were spending a summer's vacation, a volume of the works of William Ellery Channing. His sermon on the occasion of the ordination of Jared Sparks in Baltimore in 1844 opened a new horizon. Perhaps one could be free and yet have a guide freely chosen! Thus began a period of about fifteen years of so-called liberal study, thought, and preaching, which, on the whole, cannot be said to have been fruitless years for work was sincerely done and doubtless, necessary lessons learned. But measured by those inner standards, which from boyhood had subconsciously been cultivated, these were barren years.

Was this to be the fruit of mystic dreams, of Godward yearnings, of passionate longings to aid just a little in the uplift of sorrowing humanity around me? To preach once a week; duly to make my parish round of calls on elderly spinsters and the sick to whom my visits were simply what I was paid to give; to build churches to hold a handful of people; never to forget the collection, for which lapse of memory my treasurer was always scolding me, and to fill in odd hours with reading of the latest modern philosophy in order to pass it on to my unsuspecting congregation with appropriate annotations—did this round of living contain the germs of that "truth for which man ought to die"? Was it my own fault that I had missed the point and was I a fool in that I could not adjust myself to that definition of success that found its goal in a wealthy congregation, the whispered, "That was a mighty fine sermon," the annually increasing salary?

Well, anyway, suffice it to say I was desperately unhappy. I had tried the orthodox scheme; I had tried to sail the uncharted sea of—"I don't know"; I had tried the "liberal faith" and I found myself approaching spiritual bankruptcy. A balancing of Life's books showed me in debt to God and Man. It had not yet begun to dawn upon me that to be recreant to either was to be in arrears with both, and that spiritual insolvency is assured when freedom of the mind is assumed to mean liberty to follow every will-o-the-wisp of human philosophy.

It was in October of 1911 when there came to me those first stirrings of influences which were to change the course of my life. I picked up a copy of *Everybody's Magazine* from a casual bookstall and found therein a rather complete article concerning 'Abdu'l-Bahá and His projected visit to America. I shall never forget the thrill this somewhat commonplace story gave me—commonplace, I mean, in comparison with the *reality* of that story as future months were to unfold it to me. Again I heard the inner voice, which since very early youth has come to me again and again: "Come along up." I read and reread the story. Here was a Man Who had indeed found a truth for which He was not only willing to die but had died, a *living death* covering almost sixty years of torture, banishment, and imprisonment, and Who had seen many thousands of His followers willingly and joyfully face a martyr's death. And above all—O happy marvel!—here was a man who placed money where it belonged, beneath His feet. He never took up a collection!

I read and reread that glorious and tragic story and filed it in my voluminous twenty-five-volume scrapbook. There may have been a vague purpose in my mind of making that story the background of a sermon someday. To such human uses do we often put the skyey glimpses God vouchsafes us. Which is well; or would be if those celestial visions found utterance in our lives as well as through our lips.

It may have been an indication of my spiritual unrest and sense of frustration that had prompted me some months before to organize in Jersey City what we called The Brotherhood Church. It had no affiliation with my regular denominational work. No salary was attached to its service. It tried to be in fact what its name indicated: a group of brothers of the spirit aiming to express their highest ideals in service to struggling humanity. Our meetings were held in a large Masonic Hall every Sunday evening, since my suburban church held services only in the morning. How little one can estimate the great results that may flow from even slight efforts undertaken in a sincere spirit of service. It is hardly too much to say that had not this Church of Brotherhood (as ʻAbduʾl-Bahá later called it) been inaugurated and carried on for a few brief months, the Sun of Reality might not have risen for me for many years, if ever, upon this little planet.

For one of the members of the Board of Trustees was a man whom I had grown to respect and love deeply. His health was none too good and he suffered, at intervals all too short, from blinding headaches, indicating a pathological condition, which a few months later, carried him from this world. His nature was one of the humblest and sweetest I have ever known. None was too lowly or too poor to be denied his understanding love; none too casual an acquaintance to make him hesitate to seek to find and touch with healing art, the hidden springs of sorrow and distress which all conceal. His tact seemed never failing and his faith in human greatness boundless. He had no money, or little, to give. He had more, the key of universal love, which unlocks every heart.

This friend, Mr. Clarence Moore, came to me one Sunday evening just before the service was to begin and handed me some notes, saying: "I am not feeling well enough to stay this evening for I am very tired with some work I have been doing and in connection with which I want to ask your assistance." "How can I help?" I said.

"Well," he responded, "you know I have been to some extent interested in a worldwide movement, which seems to have great spiritual and social significance. Friends of mine have found in it much of value and inspiration, which so far have seemed too high and deep for me to fathom and explore. It occurred to me that your knowledge and experience in such matters might assist me to a more just appreciation. So, this afternoon I attended one of the meetings of this group in New York and made some rather full notes with the idea of submitting them to you for your criticism and opinion."*

I was dubious. There was no connection in my mind between this request and the magazine article I had lately read, and I hesitated more than a little. Oriental cults, Eastern philosophies, and the queer, supposedly idealistic movements of which there are so many, had never appealed to me. But, of course, I thanked him and on my way home in the train that night I studied his notes carefully. Interesting, I thought, heart-stirring a little, but that was about all except that I looked forward to further discussion of them with my friend.

Within a few days the mail brought to me an invitation to attend a "Bahá'í Meeting" in New York at which a woman from London, England, was to speak. At once I connected this with my friend and his notes. He had evidently given my name to someone and with this result. I was disturbed. I had no desire to be drawn into any movement or interest that might distract my attention from my legitimate work. I was on the point of throwing the card into the wastepaper basket. Only the thought of Clarence, his selfless service, his friendship and love, deterred me. I could not refuse his request that I investigate.

So I went although it entailed an evening wasted, as I thought, and a midnight return to my home, which, in my then state of health, was a not inconsiderable hardship. How slight the occasion upon which often hang great and vital issues! Suppose that I had refused to go! Nay, suppose that Clarence had allowed his physical weakness, his need of rest that Sunday afternoon, to weigh too heavily against his desire to serve; if the material had overbalanced

---

* I [Mr. Ives] came to know much later that this was just his characteristically humble and tactful way of enlisting my attention. He had long loved the teachings and his daily life was their application.

the spiritual in his mind that day I probably would not be writing these words twenty-five years later. Indeed, Sir Launfal to the contrary notwithstanding, heaven is not given away, God cannot be had for the asking unless with that asking goes all that one has.

I do not remember much of what happened at the meeting—my first Bahá'í meeting. There were readings of beautiful prayers, and I had a slight feeling of regret that they had to use a book. The friend from London talked, but nothing of what she said remains. No hymns, none of the religious trappings I had been accustomed to: but there was a spirit that attracted my heart. So when the meeting was over I asked the speaker if she could recommend someone who would come over to Jersey City and tell the story to my people. She introduced me to the chairman of the meeting, Mr. Mountfort Mills,* who, within a week or two, did give a talk in the Brotherhood Church. I remember his subject was "The Divine Springtime." One of my people sitting in front of me, for I sat in the audience during the address, seemed enthralled. She turned to me as we all rose to leave and said in a hushed voice: "There, indeed, is a man!" Her succeeding remarks indicated her meaning: A feeling of awe for the speaker and his subject. "If we could only be sure it were all true," she concluded.

Then began a period of about three months upon which I now look back as the most remarkable of my life. The divine voice calling from on high seemed constantly ringing in my ears—not that I was at all convinced of the truth underlying what I heard on every hand. In fact I did not understand half of what most of these people talked about. Sometimes I was definitely repelled and would try to put it all out of my mind. But it was no use. My heart was in a turmoil, and yet incredibly attracted. The chairman, who had given the address in the Brotherhood Church, devoted much

---

* A distinguished early American Bahá'í who served as the first chairman of the National Spiritual Assembly of the Bahá'ís of the United States and Canada.

time to me, *why* I was at a loss to understand. At his home I met several of the Bahá'í friends. And here I received my first copy of the Seven Valleys by Bahá'u'lláh. I read it on my way home that night and it stirred me beyond measure. Not one word in ten did I understand but doors seemed to be opening before me. It was like a *leit motif* from a heavenly opus of which the theme could not be guessed. Certain passages struck my heart like paeans from angelic choirs. Even the Hidden Words, by Bahá'u'lláh, given me a few days before, did not approach the core of my being as did this.

I began going over almost weekly to meetings in New York. I met more of the "friends" as I heard them designated. They certainly expressed a type of friendship new to me. I bought all the books I could find and read, read, read constantly. I could hardly think of anything else. It reflected in my sermons so that my people remarked and spoke of it. Always I had written my sermons, rather priding myself on style and ratiocination. Suddenly that all dropped away. I found myself going into the pulpit with only the preparation of prayer and meditation. And what a new meaning began to attach itself to this word *prayer!* I had always prayed after a fashion, but since religion had become a "profession," public prayer—pulpit prayer—had to a great extent displaced personal devotions. I began vaguely to understand what communion might mean.

But I was not happy. Strange to say I was more unhappy than ever. It seemed as though the very roots of my being were rent asunder. Perhaps, I thought, when 'Abdu'l-Bahá arrives He will be able to calm my restless soul. Certainly none of the proponents of His cause could do it. I had tried them all.

One day I was walking with Mountfort near his home on West End Ave. It was in February and the winter winds were chill. We walked briskly, talking of the ever enthralling subject, 'Abdu'l-Bahá's approaching visit; what He looked like; what effect His meeting had on souls; stories of contacts with Him in 'Akká and Paris. Impulsively I said:

"When 'Abdu'l-Bahá arrives I would like very much to have a talk with Him alone, without even an interpreter."

He smiled sympathetically but remarked:

"I fear you couldn't get very far without an interpreter, for 'Abdu'l-Bahá speaks little English and you, I imagine, less Persian."

I would not be dissuaded. "If He at all approaches in spiritual discernment what I hear and read of Him," I said, "we would get closer together, and I might have a better chance of understanding, even if no words were spoken. I am very tired of words," I concluded rather lamely.

This was about six weeks before 'Abdu'l-Bahá came, two months perhaps. We never referred to the subject again nor did Mountfort speak of my wish to anyone, as he afterwards assured me.

Finally the day arrived. I did not go to the steamship wharf to meet Him but I did make an effort to get at least a glimpse of Him at a gathering specially arranged for Him at the home of Bahá'í friends. A glimpse was all I succeeded in getting. The press of eager friends and curious ones was so great that it was difficult even to get inside the doors. I have only the memory of an impressive silence most unusual at such functions. In all that crowded mass of folk, so wedged together that tea drinking was almost an impossibility, though the attempt was made, there was little or no speech. A whispered word; a remark implying awe or love, was all. I strove to get where I could at least see Him—all but impossible. At last I managed to press forward where I could peep over a shoulder and so got my first glimpse of 'Abdu'l-Bahá. He was seated, a cream colored fez upon His head, from under which white hair flowed almost to His shoulders. His robe, what little I could see of it, was oriental, almost white. But these were incidentals to which I could pay little attention. The impressive thing, and what I have never forgotten, was an indefinable aspect of majesty combined with an exquisite courtesy. He was just in the moment of accepting a cup of tea from the hostess. Such gentleness, such

love emanated from Him as I had never seen. I was not emotion-
ally disturbed. Remember that at that time I had no conviction,
almost, I might say, little or no interest in what I came later to understand by the term His "Station." I was an onlooker at a scene
concerning the significance of which I was totally ignorant. Yes,
ignorant. What matter that I had read and prayed! My mind was
attracted and my heart, but inner doors were shut—and locked.
No wonder that I was unhappy. But within my soul was an urge,
a longing, that would not be stilled nor thwarted. What was it
that these people around me had that gave to their eyes such illumination, to their hearts such gladness? What connotation did
the word "wonderful" have to them that so often it was upon their
lips? I did not know, but I wanted to know as I think I had never
known the want of anything before.

The measure of that desire and the determination to discover
may be indicated in that the very next morning, early, I was at the
Hotel Ansonia where the friends had reserved rooms for Him—a
beautiful suite that 'Abdu'l-Bahá used only a few days, removing
to a simple apartment, and refusing with kindly dignity the urgent
offer of the friends to meet any expense. He said that it was not the
part of wisdom.

So before nine o'clock in the morning I was there, which meant,
since I lived some distance from New York, an early start indeed.
Already the large reception room was well-filled. Evidently others
also were conscious of a similar urge. I wondered if they too felt, as
I, a burning in the breast.

I remember as if it were yesterday the scene and my impressions.
I did not want to talk to anyone. In fact, I would not. I withdrew
to the window overlooking Broadway and turned my back upon
them all. Below me stretched the great city but I saw it not. What
was it all about? Why was I here? What did I expect from the coming interview: indeed how did I know there was to be any interview
at all? I had no appointment. Plainly all these other folk had come

expecting to see and talk with Him. Why should I expect any attention from such an evident personage?

So I was somewhat withdrawn from the others when my attention was attracted by a rustling throughout the room. A door was opening far across from me and a group was emerging and 'Abdu'l-Bahá appeared saying farewell. None had any eyes save for Him. Again I had the impression of a unique dignity and courtesy and love. The morning sunlight flooded the room to center on His robe. His fez was slightly tilted, and as I gazed, His hand, with a gesture evidently characteristic, raised and, touching, restored it to its proper place. His eyes met mine as my fascinated glance was on Him. He smiled and, with a gesture that no word but "lordly" can describe, He beckoned me. *Startled* gives no hint of my sensations. Something incredible had happened. Why to me, a stranger unknown, unheard of, should He raise that friendly hand? I glanced around. Surely it was to someone else that gesture was addressed, those eyes were smiling! But there was no one near and again I looked and again He beckoned and such understanding love enveloped me that even at that distance and with a heart still cold, a thrill ran through me as if a breeze from a divine morning had touched my brow!

Slowly I obeyed that imperative command and, as I approached the door where still He stood, He motioned others away and stretched His hand to me as if He had always known me. And, as our right hands met, with His left He indicated that all should leave the room, and He drew me in and closed the door. I remember how surprised the interpreter looked when he too was included in this general dismissal. But I had little thought then for anything but this incredible happening. I was absolutely alone with 'Abdu'l-Bahá. The halting desire expressed weeks ago was fulfilled the very moment that our eyes first met.

Still holding my hand, 'Abdu'l-Bahá walked across the room toward where, in the window, two chairs were waiting. Even then the majesty of His tread impressed me and I felt like a child led by His father, a more than earthly father, to a comforting conference. His hand still held mine and frequently His grasp tightened and held more closely. And then, for the first time, He spoke, and in my own tongue: Softly came the assurance that I was His very dear son.

What there was in these simple words that carried such conviction to my heart I cannot say. Or was it the tone of voice and the atmosphere pervading the room, filled with spiritual vibrations beyond anything I had ever known, that melted my heart almost to tears? I only know that a sense of *verity* invaded me. Here at last *was* my Father. What earthly paternal relationship could equal this? A new and exquisite emotion all but mastered me. My throat swelled. My eyes filled. I could not have spoken had life depended on a word. I followed those masterly feet like a little child.

Then we sat in the two chairs by the window: knee to knee, eye to eye. At last He looked right into me. It was the first time since our eyes had met with His first beckoning gesture that this had happened. And now nothing intervened between us and He looked at me. *He looked at me!* It seemed as though never before had anyone really seen *me*. I felt a sense of gladness that I at last was at home, and that one who knew me utterly, my Father, in truth, was alone with me.

As He looked such play of thought found reflection in His face, that if He had talked an hour not nearly so much could have been said. A little surprise, perhaps, followed swiftly by such sympathy, such understanding, such overwhelming love—it was as if His very being opened to receive me. With that, the heart within me melted and the tears flowed. I did not weep, in any ordinary sense. There was no breaking up of feature. It was as if a long-pent stream was at last undammed. Unheeded, as I looked at Him, they flowed.

He put His two thumbs to my eyes while He wiped the tears from my face; admonishing me not to cry, that one must always be happy. And He laughed—such a ringing, boyish laugh. It was as though He had discovered the most delightful joke imaginable: a divine joke that only He could appreciate.

I could not speak. We both sat perfectly silent for what seemed a long while, and gradually a great peace came to me. Then 'Abdu'l-Bahá placed His hand upon my breast saying that it was the heart that speaks. Again silence: a long, heart-enthralling silence. No word further was spoken, and all the time I was with Him not one single sound came from me. But no word was necessary from me to Him. I knew that, even then, and how I thanked God it was so.

Suddenly He leaped from His chair with another laugh as though consumed with a heavenly joy. Turning, He took me under the elbows and lifted me to my feet and swept me into His arms. Such a hug! No mere embrace! My very ribs cracked. He kissed me on both cheeks, laid His arm across my shoulders and led me to the door.

That is all. But life has never been quite the same since.

CHAPTER TWO

THE GLANCE THAT SAVED THE WORLD.
A DIVINE SINCERITY.
THE MASTERLY TEACHING METHOD.

The authorized Interpreer and Exemplar of Bahá'u'-
lláh's teachings was His eldest son 'Abdu'l-Bahá (Ser-
vant of Bahá) who was appointed by His Father
as the Center to whom all Bahá'ís, should turn for
instruction and guidance.

—Shoghi Effendi,
"The Bahá'í Faith—The World Religion"

To estimate, even to imagine, the possibilities of the human soul
is beyond man's thinking. "I am man's mystery and he is My mystery." And 'Abdu'l-Bahá says that no man can know himself since it
is impossible to look at oneself from without. Because of this, and
because men commonly tend to accept a lower estimate of their
own capacities rather than a higher, a certain heroism is essential to
high attainment. This is true, of course, when the goal is a material
one. It is not generally realized that it is much more true when the
plane of seeking is spiritual. To accept the dictum that nothing is
too good to be true, and nothing is too high to be attained, requires
a willingness to run counter to the accepted standards of men, who,
as a rule, measure their ambitions by a quite different standard.

After meeting 'Abdu'l-Bahá, life, as I have intimated, assumed a very different aspect. But in what that difference consisted I could not then determine, and after these twenty-five years I cannot now fully determine, except that a goal had emerged from the mists surrounding worthy of supreme struggle and sacrifice. I began to see, dimly indeed but clearly enough to give me hope, that even if I could not know myself, I knew with certainty that heights far beyond ever before dreamed attainable lay before me and could be reached. This was all I knew but it was much. I remember saying to myself over and over: "At last the desire of my soul is in sight." I gazed at 'Abdu'l-Bahá with a mixture of hope and despair. The world and I in turmoil and here was peace. He sat or stood, walked or talked in a world of His own, yet with beckoning hands to all who yearned and strove. It seemed to me that He stood at the heart of a whirlwind in a place of supreme quiet, or at the hypothetical perfectly still center of a rapidly revolving flywheel. I looked at this stillness, this quietude, this immeasurable calm in 'Abdu'l-Bahá and it filled me with a restless longing akin to despair. Is it any wonder I was unhappy? For I *was* desperately unhappy. Was I not in the outer circle of that raging tornado? And to attain that center of stillness meant the traversing of the storm. But to know there *was* a center: nay, to see One sitting calmly there, was a knowledge, a glimpse, never before attained. And so, another divine paradox: In my misery of doubting hope lay the first hint of divine assurance I had ever known. I remembered another arresting phrase in the Seven Valleys and said to myself: "Though I search for a hundred thousand years for the Beauty of the Friend I shall never despair for He will assuredly direct me into His way."

Not long after that great first experience with 'Abdu'l-Bahá I was again talking with Him. It was in the beautiful home of Mr. and Mrs. Kinney, a family of the friends who seemed to feel that the gift of all which they possessed was too little to express their adoring love. Entering their home, the roar of the city, the elegance and luxury of Riverside Drive, the poverty and wealth of our modern civilization, all seemed to merge into a unity of nothingness and one entered an atmosphere of Reality. Those heavenly souls who thus demonstrated beyond any words their self-dedication, had a direct influence upon my hesitating feet of which they could have had no suspicion. My heart throughout all worlds shall be filled with thankfulness to them.

In this home I had become a constant habitué. I could not keep away. One day 'Abdu'l-Bahá, the interpreter, and I were alone in one of the smaller reception rooms on the ground floor. 'Abdu'l-Bahá had been speaking of some Christian doctrine, and His interpretation of the words of Christ was so different from the accepted one, that I could not restrain an expression of remonstrance. I remember speaking with some heat:

"How is it possible to be so sure?" I asked. "No one can say with certainty what Jesus meant after all these centuries of misinterpretation and strife."

He intimated that it was quite possible.

It is indicative of my spiritual turmoil and my blindness to His station, that instead of His serenity and tone of authority impressing me as warranted, it drove me to actual impatience. "That I cannot believe" I exclaimed.

I shall never forget the glance of outraged dignity the interpreter cast upon me. It was as though he would say: "Who are you to contradict or even to question 'Abdu'l-Bahá!"

But not so did 'Abdu'l-Bahá look at me. How I thank God that it was not! He looked at me a long moment before He spoke. His calm, beautiful eyes searched my soul with such love and understanding that all my momentary heat evaporated. He smiled as winningly as a lover smiles upon his beloved, and the arms of His spirit seemed to embrace me as He said softly that I should try my way and He would try His.

It was as though a cool hand had been laid upon a fevered brow; as though a cup of nectar had been held to parched lips; as though a key had unlocked my hard-bolted, crusted, and rusted heart. The tears started and my voice trembled, "I'm sorry," I murmured.

Often since that day have I pondered on the tragic possibilities of the effect of an expression of the face. I have even thought I should like to write a book on "The Glance that Saved the World," taking as a theme the way Jesus must have looked upon Peter after the threefold denial. What could that glance have carried to the fear stricken, doubting, angry Peter? Surely not the self-righteous, dignified look in the eyes of the interpreter for 'Abdu'l-Bahá. As surely it must have been something in the nature of the expression of all-embracing love, forgiveness, and understanding with which 'Abdu'l-Bahá calmed and soothed and assured my heart.

Upon that glance, which Jesus cast upon Peter as he went to the Cross, probably hung the destinies of Christianity. Had it not been one of forgiveness and love Peter would not have gone out and "wept bitterly." Neither, in all probability, would he have died a martyr to the Cause of Him whom he denied in that moment of angry fear. Is it too much to go one step further and assert that the destinies of the world hung upon that moment of time when the eyes of Peter and His Master met and he read therein not what his soul knew he deserved but what God's mercy conferred as a bounty on His part.

Of one thing I am sure: upon that glance of 'Abdu'l-Bahá, upon that moment in which He turned upon me the searchlight of His inner being, hung my destiny throughout all the ages of immortal life. And not only my own destiny, which, after all is of slight importance compared to the hope of the world, but the destiny of the uncounted millions who throughout the coming genera-tions of men are interwoven with mine. For any thoughtful mind looking back upon so many as three-score years, must be amazed, if not horrified, by the consideration of the effect of a single care-less gesture, word, or a facial expression. Like a pebble cast into a calm pool, the ripples from that little deed spread and spread to infinity. And, as they spread, they touch the ripples from tens, scores, thousands of others' deeds, expressions, gestures, thoughts; each affected by each until one becomes conscious of the vast responsibility each soul takes upon itself by the mere fact of acting his part, living his life through one little moment of time. He sees himself a king affecting for better or worse every soul in the world, sooner or later, by the very breath he draws, the thoughts of his inmost heart. Bahá'u'lláh says somewhere that he who quickens one soul in this Day, it is as if he quickened every soul in the world.[1] Is not this His meaning?

In all of my many opportunities of meeting, of listening to, and talking with 'Abdu'l-Bahá I was impressed, and constantly more deeply impressed, with His method of teaching souls. That is the word. He did not attempt to reach the mind alone. He sought the soul, the reality of every one He met. Oh, He could be logical, even scientific in His presentation of an argument, as He demonstrated constantly in the many addresses I have heard Him give and the many more I have read. But it was not the logic of the schoolman, not the science of the classroom. His lightest word, His slightest association with a soul was shot through with an illuminating radiance that lifted the hearer to a higher plane of consciousness. Our hearts burned within us when He spoke. And He never argued, of course. Nor did He press a point. He left one free. There was never an assumption of authority, rather He was ever the personification of humility. He taught as if offering a gift to a king. He never told me what I should do, beyond suggesting that what I was doing was right. Nor did He ever tell me what I should believe. He made truth and love so beautiful and royal that the heart perforce did reverence. He showed me by His voice, manner, bearing, smile, how I should *be;* knowing that out of the pure soil of being, the good fruit of deeds and words would surely spring.

There was a strange, awe-inspiring mingling of humility and majesty, relaxation and power, in His slightest word or gesture that made me long to understand its source. What made Him so different, so immeasurably superior to any other man I had ever met?

It was to be expected that the spiritual turmoil in which my life was now submerged should have a deep effect upon the duties of my ministry. My ideals began to change almost from the moment of my first contact with 'Abdu'l-Bahá. I remember that the dearly loved young wife of one of the members of my church was suddenly taken ill about this time. I had then been under this divine influence only a few weeks. I was not a Bahá'í. I did not accept Bahá'u'lláh as the Manifestation of God. I knew very little of what I heard spoken of as the "station" of 'Abdu'l-Bahá. But I was enthralled with the vision of a spiritual beauty, a hope of spiritual attainment, which drew me as with cords of steel. I read the Hidden Words, the Seven Valleys, the Book of Assurance,[2] the beautiful prayers, constantly. So when this friend came to me as his minister and with tears asked me to pray for the recovery of his wife, saying that his physician held out little hope, that she was daily growing weaker and that his only hope was in the goodness of God, I instinctively turned to the healing prayers in the Bahá'í prayer book. Together we nine times repeated:*

Thy name is my healing, O my God, and remembrance of Thee is my remedy. Nearness to Thee is my hope, and love for Thee is my companion. Thy mercy to me is my healing and my succor in both this world and the world to come. Thou, verily, art the All-Bountiful, the All-Knowing, the All-Wise.—Bahá'u'lláh[3]

The husband knew nothing, or very little, of the Bahá'í Cause. I certainly had made no effort to explain the teachings to him. It was all too new to me to permit of that. I marveled at the time, or im-

---

* It should be noted that nowhere in the Bahá'í writings is it prescribed that one should recite this prayer nine times, and that this was simply an initiative taken by the author.

mediately after, at my temerity and at his unhesitating and grateful acceptance of the prayers. Perhaps it was with his tongue in his cheek, though he was distraught enough to grasp at any hope. Of that I can know nothing, but I do know that his wife's recovery dated from that hour and she was soon well.

I speak of this only as an illustration of the new relationships with souls that began at this time. When Christ said to His fisher disciples: "Follow Me and I will make you fishers of men," He must have meant that "following" to be a matter of spiritual conscious- ness out of which flows loving deeds. As though He would say: "Be like Me and men will love you as they love Me, and you will be able to serve men as I have served you." At any rate that is what 'Abdu'l- Bahá was constantly showing me, that the only way I could teach men the Way of Life was by walking therein myself. "I am the Way."

I asked 'Abdu'l-Bahá one day: "Why should I believe in Bahá'u'lláh?"

He looked long and searchingly as it seemed into my very soul. The silence deepened. He did not answer. In that silence I had time to consider why I had asked the question, and dimly I began to see that only I myself could supply the reason. After all, why should I believe in anyone or anything except as a means, an incentive, a dynamic for the securing of a fuller, deeper, more perfect life? Does the cabinet-maker's apprentice ask himself why he should believe in the master woodworker? He wants to know how to make these raw materials into things of beauty and usefulness. He *must* believe in anyone who can show him how to do that, providing he first has faith in his own capacity. I had the stuff of life. Was Bahá'u'lláh the Master Workman? If He were I knew that I would follow, even though through blood and tears. But how could I *know?*

I wondered why 'Abdu'l-Bahá kept silence so long. Yet was it silence? That stillness held more than words. At last He spoke. He said that the work of a Christian minister is most important. When you preach or pray or teach your people, your heart must be filled with love for them and love for God. And you must be sincere— *very sincere.*

He spoke in Persian, the interpreter translating fluently and beautifully. But no one could interpret that divine voice. He spoke, indeed, as never mere man spake. One listened entranced and understood inwardly even before the interpreter opened his mouth. It was as though the English skimmed the surface: the voice, the eyes, the smile of 'Abdu'l-Bahá taught the heart to probe the depths. He continued, to the effect that:

> One can never be sincere enough until his heart is entirely severed from attachment to the things of this world. One should not preach love and have a loveless heart, nor preach purity and harbor impure thoughts. Nor preach peace and be at inward strife.

He paused and added with a sort of humorous sadness: that He had known ministers who did this. My guilty conscience acquiesced. So had I.

It was not until many months later that I realized that He had answered my question. Certainly I was brought nearer to faith in Bahá'u'lláh as life's Master Workman. Surely this was a glorious hint as to how the stuff of life could be made into things of beauty and worth. Just for an instant I touched the garment of His majesty, but only for an instant. The doors swung quickly to again and left me out. These days and weeks of alternating light and darkness, hope and despair, were black indeed. Yet, strange to say, I gloried in the depths. They were at least *real*. For the first time I realized the value, the imperative need, of spiritual suffering. The throes of parturition must always precede birth.

I remember as though it were yesterday another illustration of 'Abdu'l-Bahá's divine technique. I was not at all well that summer. A relapse was threatening a return of a condition that had necessitated a major operation the year before. My nervous condition made me consider breaking the habit of smoking, which had been with me all my adult life. I had always prided myself on the ability to break the habit at any time. In fact I had several times cut off the use of tobacco for a period of many months. But this time to my surprise and chagrin I found my nerves and will in such a condition that after two or three days the craving became too much for me.

Finally it occurred to me to ask the assistance of 'Abdu'l-Bahá. I had read His beautiful Tablet beginning: "O ye pure friends of God!" in which He glorified personal cleanliness and urged the avoidance of anything tending toward habits of self-indulgence. "Surely," I said to myself, "He will tell me how to overcome this habit."

So, when I next saw Him I told Him all about it. It was like a child confessing to His mother, and my voice trailed away to embarrassed silence after only the fewest of words. But He understood, indeed much better than I did. Again I was conscious of an embracing, understanding love as He regarded me. After a moment He asked quietly, how much I smoked.

I told him.

He said He did not think that would hurt me, that the men in the Orient smoked all the time, that their hair and beards and clothing became saturated, and often very offensive. But that I did not do this, and at my age and having been accustomed to it for so many years, He did not think that I should let it trouble me at all. His gentle eyes and smile seemed to hold a twinkle that recalled my impression of His enjoyment of a divine joke.

I was somewhat overwhelmed. Not a dissertation on the evils of habit; not an explanation of the bad effects on health; not a summoning of my will power to overcome desire, rather a Charter of Freedom did He present to me. I did not understand, but it was a great relief for somehow I knew that this was wise advice. So immediately that inner conflict was stilled and I enjoyed my smoke with no smitings of conscience. But two days after this conversation I found the desire for tobacco had entirely left me and I did not smoke again for seven years.

Love is the Portal to Freedom. This great truth began to dawn upon me—not only freedom to the one who loves, but freedom also to the one upon whom this divine love is bestowed. I have mentioned several times the impression He always made upon me of an all-embracing love. How rarely we receive such an impression from those around us, even from our nearest and dearest, we all know. All our human love seems based upon self, and even its highest expression is limited to one or to a very few. Not so was the love that radiated from 'Abdu'l-Bahá. Like the sun it poured upon all alike and, like it, also warmed and gave new life to all it touched.

In my experience in the Christian ministry I had been accustomed often to speak of the love of God. All through my life since, as a boy of fifteen I had experienced the thrilling gift of "conversion," so-called (in which, literally, the heavens had opened, a great light shone, and a voice from the world unseen called me to renunciation and the life of the spirit), I had heard and spoken much of the love of God. I now realized that I had never before even known what the words meant.

About this time I first heard the now familiar story of 'Abdu'l-Bahá's answer to one who asked Him why it was that those who came from His presence possessed a shining face. He said, with that sublime smile and humble gesture of the hands, which once seen may never be forgotten, that if it were so it must be because He saw in every face the face of His Heavenly Father.

Ponder this answer. Deeply search the depths of these simple words, for here may be discerned the meaning of the "love of God" and the cause of its transforming power. One may readily understand why the lover's face should glow with heavenly radiance. Surely one's whole being would be transformed once the lamp of cosmic love was ignited in the heart. But why should it cause the face of the seeker, the estranged, the sinful, upon whom the love is turned, also to become radiant?

We find the answer in another of 'Abdu'l-Bahá's comprehensive, authoritative sayings:[4]

"Dost thou desire to love God? Love thy fellow men, for in them ye see the image and likeness of God."

But it requires the penetrating eye of a more than personal, individual, limited, love to see God's face in the face of saint and sinner alike. Must it not require, to some degree at least, that all-embracing love that Christ showered upon all alike, to enable us to see the face of our Heavenly Father reflected in the faces of our brother men? This must be what our Lord meant when He said:

"A new commandment I give unto you that ye love one another as I have loved you."

A new commandment indeed, and how basely neglected—let the condition of our pseudo-Christian civilization bear witness.

About this time I was present at an interview sought by a Unitarian clergyman, who was preparing an article on the Bahá'í Cause for the *North American Review*. Here again I saw this universal, cosmic love illustrated. This minister was quite advanced in age. He has since passed from this world and now, we may hope, has a clearer vision of the reality of love and truth than he seemed to have discovered here. It was incredible to me, even then, that any soul could be so impervious to the influence emanating from 'Abdu'l-Bahá. The Master sat quite silent throughout the interview, listening with unwearied attention to the long hypothetical questions of the reverend doctor. They related entirely to the history of the Bahá'í Cause; its early dissensions; its relation to the Muhammadan priesthood and teachings. 'Abdu'l-Bahá answered mainly in monosyllables. He never flagged in interest but it seemed to be more an interest in the questioner than in his questions. He sat perfectly relaxed—His hands in His lap with palms upward, as was characteristic of Him. He looked at the interviewer with that indescribable expression of understanding love that never failed. His face was radiant with an inner flame.

The doctor talked on and on. I grew more and more impatient. I was ashamed of, and for, him. Why did not 'Abdu'l-Bahá recognize the superficial nature underlying all these questions? Could

He not see that their object was only to gain substantiation for a critically adverse magazine article for the writing of which a substantial check might be anticipated? Why was not the interview cut short and the talker dismissed? But if others in the group grew impatient, 'Abdu'l-Bahá did not. He encouraged the doctor to express himself fully. If the speaker flagged for a moment 'Abdu'l-Bahá spoke briefly in reply to a question and then waited courteously for him to continue.

At last the reverend doctor paused. There was silence for a moment and then that softly resonant voice filled the room. Sentence by sentence the interpreter translated. He spoke of "His Holiness Christ," of His love for all men, strong even unto the Cross; of the high station of the Christian ministry "to which you, my dear son, have been called"; of the need that men called to this station should "characterize themselves with the characteristics of God" in order that their people should be attracted to the divine life, for none can resist the expression in one's life of the attributes of God. It is a key which unlocks every heart. He spoke, too, of the coming Kingdom of God on earth for which Christ had told us to pray and, which, in accordance with His promise, Bahá'u'lláh, the Father, had come to this world to establish.

Within five minutes His questioner had become humble, for the moment, at least, a disciple at His feet. He seemed to have been transported to another world, as indeed we all were. His face shone faintly as though he had received an inner illumination. Then 'Abdu'l-Bahá rose. We all rose with Him in body as we had risen with Him in spirit. He lovingly embraced the doctor and led him toward the door. At the threshold He paused. His eyes had lighted upon a large bunch of American Beauty roses that one of the friends had brought to Him that morning. There were at least two dozen of them, perhaps three. There were so many and their stems so long that they had been placed in an earthenware umbrella stand. We all had noticed their beauty and fragrance.

No sooner had 'Abdu'l-Bahá's eyes lighted upon them than He laughed aloud; His boyish hearty laughter rang through the room. He stooped, gathered the whole bunch in His arms, straightened and placed them all in the arms of His visitor. Never shall I forget that round, bespectacled, gray head above that immense bunch of lovely flowers—so surprised, so radiant, so humble, so transformed. Ah! 'Abdu'l-Bahá knew how to teach the love of God!

CHAPTER THREE

True Wealth, Power, and Freedom. The Table of 'Abdu'l-Bahá. Very Great Things. "Are You Interested In Renunciation?"

Illumine, O my Lord, the eyes of Thy servants, and brighten their hearts with the splendors of the light of Thy knowledge, that they may apprehend the greatness of this most sublime station, and recognize this most luminous Horizon, that haply the clamor of men may fail to deter them from turning their gaze towards the effulgent light of Thy unity, and to hinder them from setting their faces toward the Horizon of detachment.

—Bahá'u'lláh, Prayers and Meditations, p. 275

The home to which I have before referred, where 'Abdu'l-Bahá spent most of His time during His stay in New York, was the rendezvous of all the friends, and at all times, day or night, there they could be found clustering like bees around the celestial flower garden. One beautiful spring day I dropped in there, drawn by the same attraction.

One cannot help making the attempt toward analyzing the reason for this attraction, futile though it may be. Would it be possible for the moth to determine *why* it hovers around the candle, even though its wings be singed? Or for one to say *why* the cold earth of spring responds with beauty and abundance to the bounty of the sun? To man, however, is given intelligence denied to bee and soil. The miner knows why he toils for gold or precious stones. The diver knows why he braves the depths to seek the pearl. They bear in their minds the vision of the good things of life represented by the treasure they seek. The imagination of the lonely prospector is stirred by the dream of the vast fortune, which his probing look may at any moment uncover. The wealth of sea and mine and marketplace represent to men power, leisure, freedom; and these they ardently desire. Yet here in this Man I saw personified such power, such leisure, such freedom as no material wealth ever confers upon its possessor. None of the outward appurtenances of material wealth did He possess. All His life had been spent in prison and exile. He bore still upon His body the marks of man's cruelty, yet there were no signs of His ever having been other than free, and evidently it was a freedom that no earthly wealth ever bestows. And He seemed never to be hurried. Amidst the rushing turmoil of New York He walked as calmly as if on a lofty plateau, far removed from the tumult and the shouting. Yet He never stood aloof. Always His interest in people and events was keen, especially in people. *Souls* was the term He always used. He was ever at the service of any or all who needed Him. From five o'clock in the morning frequently until long after midnight He was actively engaged in service, yet no evidence of haste or stress ever could be seen in Him. "Nothing is too much trouble when one loves," He had been heard to say, "and there is always time."

Is it any wonder that we were attracted? But for me the attraction was not enough. I was like the prospector drawn by visions of wealth to seek its fabulous source. Just a sip of that celestial wine had caused to spring up in my heart a passionate desire to seek the Holy Grail.

It was mid-afternoon when I arrived at the house, for I had purposely timed my arrival so that it should not be at the luncheon hour, for hospitable as were the souls of these dedicated ones, and however flexible their dining table, I knew the size of their household and the great number of probably uninvited, but always welcome, guests. There were many bees. But I had not counted on the irregularity of 'Abdu'l-Bahá's meal times and now, at half-past three or four o'clock in the afternoon I heard, as I softly ascended the stairway, the unmistakable sounds of a large group busy in the dining room. The last thing I desired was to walk in upon such a gathering unexpectedly, so I very quietly crept through the upper hall and through the drawing room into a little alcove as far from the dining room as I could get. I am very sure that no one saw me. But I had no sooner picked up a magazine and settled myself to wait patiently until the meal should be over, than 'Abdu'l-Bahá's ringing, challenging voice pealed like a bell through the large rooms. He called my name: "Mr. Ives, Mr. Ives, come, come." There could be no hesitation when He summoned, but as I rose and walked slowly back into the long dining room, set T-shape to the drawing room, I was amazed, wondering how He could have known so surely and so quickly that I was there. There had been no opportunity for Him to have been told, and, anyhow I had let myself in at the unlocked door and, as I have said, no one had seen me ascend the stairs. Yet here I was evidently an expected, if not an invited guest. Even a place was there for me. At any rate I have no remembrance of any of the usual fuss of "setting a place." 'Abdu'l-Bahá embraced me and set me at His right hand.

It is most difficult to describe at all adequately such an experience in such a Presence without becoming rhapsodical. There were perhaps thirty people at the table and such joyous exultation was on every face that the whole room seemed strangely vibrant. 'Abdu'l-Bahá served me with His own hands most bountifully, urging me to eat, eat, be happy. He Himself did not eat but paced regally around the table, talking, smiling, serving. He told stories of the East, His hands gesturing with that graceful, rhythmic, upward motion so characteristic and so indescribable. I had no desire for food, at least not for the food on my plate, but 'Abdu'l-Bahá was insistent, repeating that I must eat; that it was good food, good food. And His laughter seemed to add a divine significance to the words. A phrase I had read somewhere in the writings came into my mind: "The cup of significances passed by the Hand of the Divine Servant."[5] What was this food served at the table of 'Abdu'l-Bahá? Of course I must eat. And I did.

It was not many days after that when there occurred one of the most poignantly remembered incidents. Ever since I had first read a sentence in the "Prayer for Inspiration" it had rung in my mind with insistent questioning. "Prevent me not from turning to the Horizon of renunciation."[6] What has renunciation to do with inspiration? I wondered. Why should I pray for the gift of renunciation? Renounce the world? That was an ascetic concept. It smacked of papacy and the monkish cell. What had this modern world to do with renunciation? Yet across the ages came a voice: *"If a man love father or mother, wife or child more than Me he is not worthy of Me."* My mind rebelled but my heart responded. I thank God for that. I resolved that I must know more of this matter.

So one cold spring day, a strong east wind blowing, I made a special journey to ask 'Abdu'l-Bahá about renunciation. I found the house at Ninety-sixth Street almost deserted. It seemed that 'Abdu'l-Bahá was spending a day or two at the home of one of the friends on Seventy-eighth Street and so I walked there and found Him on the point of returning to the home I had just left. But I was too intent on my mission to allow difficulties to interfere. I sought one of the Persian friends and, pointing to the passage in the little volume I carried in my pocket, I asked him if he would request 'Abdu'l-Bahá to speak to me for a few moments on this subject, and I read it to him so that there should be no mistake: "Prevent me not from turning to the Horizon of renunciation."

Returning, he handed me the book saying that 'Abdu'l-Bahá requested that I walk with Him back to Ninety-sixth Street, and He would talk with me on the way.

I recall that there was quite a little procession of us, a dozen or
so, mostly composed of the Persian friends but a few others; Lua
Getsinger was one, I remember. The east wind was penetrating.
I buttoned my coat closely with a little shiver. But 'Abdu'l-Bahá
strode along with his 'abá (cloak) floating in the wind. He looked
at me as we walked together at the head of the little group, with
a slightly quizzical glance. He said that I seemed cold, a slightly
amused glance accompanying the words, and I unaccountably felt
a little disturbed. Why should I not feel cold? Could one be expected to live even above the weather? But this slight remark was
indicative. Always His slightest word affected me as a summons.
"Come up higher!" He seemed to say.

As we walked a few paces ahead of the others He talked at length
about Horizons—of how the Sun of Reality, like the physical sun,
rose at different points, the Sun of Moses at one point, the Sun of
Jesus at another, the Sun of Muhammad, the Sun of Bahá'u'lláh
at still others. . . . Always the same Sun, though the rising points
varied greatly. Always we must look for the light of the Sun, He
said, and not keep our eyes so firmly fixed on its last point of rising
that we fail to see its glory when it rises in the new Spiritual Springtime. Once or twice He stopped and, with His stick, drew on the
sidewalk an imaginary horizon and indicated the rising points of
the sun. A strange sight it must have been to the casual passerby.

I was greatly disappointed. I had heard Him speak on this subject and had read about it in *Some Answered Questions*. It was not of
horizons I wanted to hear, but of renunciation. And I was deeply
depressed also because I felt that He should have known my desire
for light on this subject, and responded to my longing even if I had
not been so explicit in my request; but I had been most explicit.
As we approached our destination He became silent. My disappointment had long since merged into a great content. Was it not
enough to be with Him? What, after all, could He tell me about
renunciation that was not already in my own heart? Perhaps the

way to learn about it was by doing, and I might begin by giving up the longing to have Him talk to me about it. Truly, as the outer silence deepened, my heart burned within me as He talked with me on the way.

We came at last to the steps leading up to the entrance door. 'Abdu'l-Bahá paused with one foot resting on the lower step while the little group slowly passed Him and entered the house. 'Abdu'l-Bahá made as if to follow, but instead He turned and, looking down at me from the little elevation of the step, with that subtle meaning in eyes and voice, which seemed to accompany His slightest word, and which to me was always so unfathomable and so alluring, He said that I must always remember that this is a day of great things, very great things.

I was speechless. It was not for me to answer. I did not have the faintest inkling of what lay behind the words, the resonant voice, that penetrating glance. Then He turned and again made as if to ascend but again He paused and turned His now luminous face toward me. My foot was raised to follow but as He turned, I, of course, paused also and hung uncertainly between rest and motion.

He repeated, saying to me so impressively, so earnestly, that I must never forget this, that *this is a day for very great things.*

What could He mean? What deep significance lay behind these simple words? Why should He speak so to me? Had it anything to do with that still alluring thought of renunciation?

Again 'Abdu'l-Bahá turned to ascend and I made to follow; but for the third time He paused and, turning, as it seemed, the full light of His spirit upon me He said again, but this time in what seemed like a voice of thunder, with literally flashing eyes and emphatically raised hand: that I should remember His words that This is a Day for *very great things*—VERY GREAT THINGS. These last three words rang out like a trumpet call. The long, deserted city block seemed to echo them. I was overwhelmed. I seemed to dwindle, almost to shrivel, where I stood, as that beautifully dominant figure, that commanding and appealing voice, surrounded me like a sea, and blotted out for the moment, at least, all the petty world and my petty self with it. Who and what was I to be summoned to accomplish great things, very great things? I did not even know what things were great in this world awry with misbegotten emphases.

After what seemed a very long moment, in which His burning eyes probed my soul, He gently smiled. The great moment had passed. He was again the courteous, kindly, humble host, the Father whom I thought I knew. He touched His fez* so that it stood at what I called the humorous angle, and a slightly quizzical smile was around His mouth as He rapidly ascended the steps and entered the open door. I followed closely. We passed through the few steps of the hall to the stairs. I remember the wondering, slightly envious, glances that followed me as I followed 'Abdu'l-Bahá up the stairs. The upper hall was empty and 'Abdu'l-Bahá swept through it and up another flight to His room, a large front room on the third floor. And still I followed. I have often marveled since at my temerity. Had I known more or felt less I never should have dared. It is said that fools rush in where angels fear to tread. Perhaps that is the way that fools are cured of their folly.

We came to the door of 'Abdu'l-Bahá's room. He had not invited me there, nor had He looked once behind Him to see that I was following, and it was with much inward trepidation that I paused at the threshold as He entered the room. Would He be displeased? Had I overstepped the bounds of the respect due 'Abdu'l-Bahá? Had I been lacking in due humility? But my heart was humility itself—He must know that. He swung the door wide, and turning, beckoned me in.

Again I was alone with 'Abdu'l-Bahá. There was the bed in which He slept, the chair in which He sat. The late afternoon sunlight lay palely across the floor, but I saw nothing. I was conscious only of

---

* Head covering.

Him and that I was alone with Him. The room was very still. No sound came from the street nor from the lower rooms. The silence deepened as He regarded me with that loving, all-embracing, all-understanding look that always melted my heart. A deep content and happiness flooded my being. A little flame seemed lit within my breast. And then 'Abdu'l-Bahá spoke: He simply asked me if I were interested in renunciation.

Nothing could have been more unexpected. I had entirely forgotten the question that had so engrossed my thoughts an hour since. Or was it that in that hour, during which the word *renunciation* had not been mentioned, all that I wished or needed to know about it had been vouchsafed me? I had no words to answer His question. Was I interested? I could not say I was and I would not say I was not. I stood before Him silent while His whole being seemed to reach out to embrace me. Then His arm was around me and He led me to the door. I left His presence with my soul treading the heights. I felt as though I had been admitted, for the moment at least, into the ranks of the martyrs. And it was a goodly fellowship indeed. During all the long years of renunciation that followed, the memory of that walk with Him; my disappointment that He had not understood; His ringing challenge: This is a Day for *very great things;* my following Him up those long stairs without even knowing whether He wished me to or not, and then the question wrapped in that sublime love: "Are you interested in renunciation?," has risen before me, a comforting and inspiring challenge. Indeed I *was* interested and my interest has never flagged from that day to this. But I never dreamed that renunciation could be so glorious.

CHAPTER FOUR

THE ATTRACTION OF PERFECTION.
THE BOYS FROM THE BOWERY.
A BLACK ROSE AND A BLACK SWEET.

And finally there emerges, though on a plane of its own and in a category entirely apart from the one occupied by the twin Figures that preceded Him (the Báb and Bahá'u'lláh), the vibrant, the magnetic personality of 'Abdu'l-Bahá, reflecting to a degree that no man, however exalted his station, can hope to rival, the glory and power with which They who are the Manifestations of God are alone endowed.
　　　　　　　　　　　　　　　—Shoghi Effendi,
　　　　　The World Order of Bahá'u'lláh, pp. 97–98

During one of the talks given by 'Abdu'l-Bahá to a comparatively small group of the more intimate friends, I sat beside Him on a small sofa. For most of the hour, while He talked and answered questions, He held my hand in His or rested it lightly upon my knee. There flowed from Him to me during that marvelous contact a constant stream of power. The remembrance of this experience has brought to me through the years, at higher moments of insight, thoughts difficult to express. "Words cannot step into that Court." When 'Abdu'l-Bahá says that "there is a Power in this Cause far transcending the ken of men and angels," what does He mean in terms applicable to our everyday human experience, if not that the world of reality is a world of such power as this world has never known? When mankind learns how to become a channel for that power, as He always was and is, instead of attempting to mop it up for one's own exclusive use, then indeed this world will become a garden and a paradise. Certainly I felt that transcendent power flowing from Him to me; and Mr. Mountfort Mills once told me that he had the same experience when sitting close to 'Abdu'l-Bahá during an automobile ride. He said it was like being charged by a divine battery.

I speak of this only because it is another illustration of the effect 'Abdu'l-Bahá's presence always had on me. I could not be near Him without surges of almost irresistible emotion sweeping through me. Sometimes the effects of this emotion were apparent, but not always. I once spoke of this to 'Abdu'l-Bahá, apologetically referring to my "childish weakness." He said that such tears were the pearls of the heart.

It is not unusual for deep emotions to be stirred when the eye is satisfied by a noble picture, a glorious sunset, or a peach orchard in full bloom. Or when the ear is entranced by the genius of a Beethoven, a Bach, a Mendelssohn. To the eye or ear trained to detect subtle harmonies of color, composition and tone, a chord is struck by transcendent beauty, which stirs the depths. How much more must this be true when the eye, the ear, the heart are filled with the vision of human perfection.

Here in 'Abdu'l-Bahá I saw that for which all my life I had longed —perfection in word and deed—a beauty which no line or tone could ever depict; a harmony which resounded to my inner ear like a mighty symphony; a reposeful power such as is hinted at in the *Moses* of Michael Angelo, or the *Thinker* of Rodin. In 'Abdu'l-Bahá it was not a hint I got, it was the perfection of all that the hungry heart desired. I have heard of instances in the Orient of believers who entered His presence for the first time being swept by such irresistible tides of emotion that they would seem to dissolve in tears. I cannot wonder. Here I saw and felt and heard a simplicity merging into power; a humility, which sat on His brow like a kingly crown; a purity, which never famished, and, above all, truth personified—the very Spirit of Truth enshrined in a human temple. It was utter satisfaction to my soul simply to be near Him.

Perhaps there was also a reason for my emotion in the despair lying ever deep within; for to me it could never be enough merely to contemplate such perfection. A voice continually cried within me: "You must never rest until you have clothed yourself in the attributes of God." I seemed to hear in every word He spoke the words of Jesus: *"You must be perfect even as your Father in heaven is perfect."* These had always been more or less only words to me. I began now dimly to hope that they might really mean exactly what they said. And this became certainty when I read for the first of many times these wonderful words from Bahá'u'lláh's Tablet to the Pope:

> If ye follow Me, ye shall behold that which ye were promised, and I will make you My companions in the dominion of My majesty and the intimates of My beauty in the heaven of My power forevermore.[7]

Under the influence of such tremendous thoughts as these I one day asked 'Abdu'l-Bahá how it could ever be possible for me, deep in the mass of weak and selfish humanity, ever to hope to attain when the goal was so high and great. He said that it is to be accomplished little by little; little by little. And I thought to myself, I have all eternity for this journey from self to God. The thing to do is to get started.

Toward the latter part of April, late one Sunday afternoon, I was again at the home where so many wonderful hours had been spent. It had become almost a habit, when the service at my church was over and dinner dispatched, to hasten in to New York and spend the rest of the day and evening at this home. Sometimes I would have an opportunity to speak to 'Abdu'l-Bahá, but usually I must be content with a glimpse of Him, or with listening to Him while He spoke to a small group. This particular afternoon, however, was destined to be a red-letter day. I was standing alone at one of the windows looking out upon the street when I was startled by seeing a large group of boys come rushing up the steps. There seemed twenty or thirty of them. And they were not what one would call representatives of the cultured class. In fact, they were a noisy and not-too-well-dressed lot of urchins, but spruce and clean as if for an event. They came up the steps with a stamping of feet and loud talk, and I heard them being ushered in and up the stairs.

I turned to Mrs. Kinney, who was standing near. "What is the meaning of all this?" I asked.

"Oh, this is really the most surprising thing," she exclaimed, "I asked them to come today, but I hardly expected that they would."

It seemed that a few days before, 'Abdu'l-Bahá had gone to the Bowery Mission to speak to several hundred of New York's wretched poor. As usual, with Him went a large group of the Persian and American friends, and it made a unique spectacle as this party of Orientals in flowing robes and strange headgear made its way through the East Side. Not unnaturally, a number of boys gathered in their train and soon they became a little too vocal in their expression. As I remember, even some venturesome ones called names and threw sticks. As my Hostess told the story, she said: "I could not bear to hear 'Abdu'l-Bahá so treated and dropped behind the others for a moment to speak to them. In a few words, I told them Who He was; that He was a very Holy Man who had spent many years in exile and prison because of His love for truth and for men, and that now He was on His way to speak to the poor men at the Bowery Mission."

"Can't we go too?" one who seemed to be the leader asked. "I think that would be impossible," she told them, "but if you come to my home next Sunday," and she gave them the address, "I will arrange for you to see Him." So here they were. We followed them up the stairs and into 'Abdu'l-Bahá's own room. I was just in time to see the last half-dozen of the group entering the room.

'Abdu'l-Bahá was standing at the door and He greeted each boy as he came in; sometimes with a handclasp, sometimes with an arm around a shoulder, but always with such smiles and laughter it almost seemed that He was a boy with them. Certainly there was no suggestion of stiffness on their part, or awkwardness in their unaccustomed surroundings. Among the last to enter the room was a colored lad of about thirteen years. He was quite dark and, being the only boy of his race among them, he evidently feared that he might not be welcome. When 'Abdu'l-Bahá saw him His face lighted up with a heavenly smile. He raised His hand with a gesture of princely welcome and exclaimed in a loud voice so that none could fail to hear; that here was a black rose.

The room fell into instant silence. The black face became illumined with a happiness and love hardly of this world. The other boys looked at him with new eyes. I venture to say that he had been called a black—many things, but never before a black rose.

This significant incident had given to the whole occasion a new complexion. The atmosphere of the room seemed now charged with subtle vibrations felt by every soul. The boys, while losing nothing of their ease and simplicity, were graver and more intent upon 'Abdu'l-Bahá, and I caught them glancing again and again at the colored boy with very thoughtful eyes. To the few of the friends in the room the scene brought visions of a new world in which every soul would be recognized and treated as a child of God. I thought: What would happen to New York if these boys could carry away such a keen remembrance of this experience that throughout their lives, whenever they encountered any representatives of the many races and colors to be found in that great city, they would think of them and treat them as "different colored flowers in the Garden of God." The freedom from just this one prejudice in the minds and hearts of this score or more of souls would unquestionably bring happiness and freedom from rancor to thousands of hearts. How simple and easy to be kind, I thought, and how hardly we learn.

When His visitors had arrived, 'Abdu'l-Bahá had sent out for some candy and now it appeared, a great five pound box of expensive mixed chocolates. It was unwrapped and 'Abdu'l-Bahá walked with it around the circle of boys, dipping His hand into the box and placing a large handful in the hands of each, with a word and smile for everyone. He then returned to the table at which He had been sitting, and laying down the box, which now had only a few pieces in it, He picked from it a long chocolate nougat; it was very black. He looked at it a moment and then around at the group of boys who were watching Him intently and expectantly. Without a word, He walked across the room to where the colored boy was sitting, and, still without speaking, but with a humorously piercing glance that swept the group, laid the chocolate against the black cheek. His face was radiant as He laid His arm around the shoulder of the boy and that radiance seemed to fill the room. No words were necessary to convey His meaning, and there could be no doubt that all the boys caught it.

You see, He seemed to say, that he is not only a black flower, but also a black sweet. You eat black chocolates and find them good: perhaps you would find this black brother of yours good also if you once taste his sweetness.

Again that awed hush fell upon the room. Again the boys all looked with real wonder at the colored boy as if they had never seen him before, which indeed was true. And as for the boy himself, upon whom all eyes were now fixed, he seemed perfectly unconscious of all but 'Abdu'l-Bahá. Upon Him his eyes were fastened with an adoring, blissful look such as I had never seen upon any face. For the moment he was transformed. The reality of his being had been brought to the surface and the angel he really was revealed.

I left the house with many deep thoughts crowding my heart. Who was this man? Why did He have such power over souls? He made no pretensions of goodness. He did not preach; oh, never!

Not even by the faintest implication did He ever intimate that one should be otherwise than what he was: yet somehow He showed us worlds of beauty and grandeur that tore our hearts with longing to attain, and made us loathe the round of so-called life to which we were bound. I did not know what to think of it all, but I did know, even then, that I loved Him as I had never dreamed of love. I did not believe as those around me did. Indeed, I hardly ever thought of what their many words concerning His "station" sought to convey. I was not interested in that at all, it seems. But I certainly did believe that He held a secret of life, which I would give my life to discover for myself.

I spent myself in prayer that night. I felt that I had never really prayed before. I am not given to what is called occult, or mystic experiences, but as I prayed that night there were surely presences in the room. I heard rustlings and little whisperings. A new and wonderful world opened before me from that night.

CHAPTER FIVE

A Leaf in the Breeze of the Will Of God.
"My Throne is My Mat."
Inscription in The Seven Valleys.
The Power of the Word of God.

Every word that proceedeth out of the mouth of God is endowed with such potency as can instill new life into every human frame, if ye be of them that comprehend this truth. All the wondrous works ye behold in this world have been manifested through the operation of His supreme and most exalted Will, His wondrous and inflexible Purpose.

—Bahá'u'lláh,
Gleanings from the Writings of Bahá'u'lláh, no. 74.1

"We should count time by heart throbs." When I recall that all so far recounted occurred within the first three weeks after my meeting with 'Abdu'l-Bahá, it seems incredible. In those few days life had taken on an entirely new meaning. I felt like a spiritual Columbus exploring the uncharted oceans of God. New lands had been discovered upon which I hardly had courage to set foot. Heights and depths of inner experience had been touched of which heretofore I had never dreamed. Truly, many times I had "packed eternity into an hour, or stretched an hour to eternity."

One day, about the first of May of that momentous year, I asked 'Abdu'l-Bahá if He could arrange to speak to my congregation at the Brotherhood Church. He considered a moment, then said smilingly: God willing. This was to me a new way of responding to such a request. A ripple of wonderment crossed my mind as to how many engagements for public speakers would be made in our modern world if both parties referred the decision to the will of God before its ratification. How could I arrange the necessary preliminaries on such an uncertainty? How was I to know whether God was willing or not? 'Abdu'l-Bahá noticed my hesitation and waited courteously for me to speak. Rather haltingly I said: "It will be necessary for me to know the date a few days in advance in order to be able to make the necessary public announcements."

He asked me how long before I would need to know.

"A week or ten days would be sufficient, I think."

He said I should ask Him then.

And so a week later I asked Him if Sunday evening, May 19, would be convenient for Him. He said: "Very good," and so it was arranged.

This incident gave me renewed food for thought. I got a little glimpse of the source of the Master's mingled relaxation and power. He was never tense or hurried; never at a loss for word or act. He seldom used the first person singular. I have heard Him in His public talks refer to 'Abdu'l-Bahá as if that person were entirely distinct from the speaker. Any reference to the ego, He once remarked to a small group of the New York friends, any use of "I," "Me," "Mine," will in the future be considered as profanity.

The phrase "God willing" was constantly upon His lips. If one could ask a leaf in the clutch of autumn winds whither it was going, would it not answer, if it could, "I know and care not. I go where God's breezes blow me." In truth 'Abdu'l-Bahá was a "leaf in the breeze of the Will of God." Unquestionably this was one of the reasons for that atmosphere of majesty, which always attended

Him, and which no one entering His presence could fail to note. How natural to be king-like when one is under the immediate inspiration and guidance of the King of kings! The gestures, posture, gait of the Master were ever king-like.

Mr. Mills, the friend to whose influence and tactfulness I am most indebted for my deepening interest, and who had been the cause of my first meeting 'Abdu'l-Bahá, once remarked to me that he had seen only two men of whom it could truthfully be said that "He walks like a king." One was King Edward VII; the other was 'Abdu'l-Bahá. Yet while the former had been trained from infancy to expect deference, obedience, humility from millions of subjects, whose allegiance is now transferred to his grandson, the latter from the age of seven years had been trained in the glorious school of Martyrdom. Not His had been a home in palaces and rest upon beds of ease. Rather, His had been the portion of a prisoner and an exile. His bed the floor of the prison morgue, which He chose as the only place in the fortress where He could be alone and pray, His resting place too often the stocks and chains. Yet at any moment He could have been free to return to the life of wealth and ease to which He had been born, would He but renounce His allegiance to truth and the Glory of God (Bahá'u'lláh) reflected in the earthly Temple of His Father.

> "My throne is my mat!" He said, "My glorious crown is my servitude toward God! My standard is the commemoration of my Lord! My hosts are the knowledge of my Master! My sword is the guidance of God! My dominion is my humility, my submissiveness, my lowliness, my abasement, my supplication and my beseeching unto God—this is that permanent reign which no one is able to dispute, gainsay or usurp!"[8]

He lived to see many thousands die as martyrs for the truth for which He had sacrificed His life, and millions of the living render to

Him an homage "which kings might envy and emperors sigh for in vain."[9] No wonder He walked like a king, rather like a King of kings.

I think it was in connection with the plans for His approaching visit to the Brotherhood Church that He said to me one day that He had noticed that many ministers and public speakers prepare their addresses in advance, often committing them to memory and speaking the same words to many different audiences. He paused and looked at me a little humorously, a little sadly, and added that He wondered how they can be sure of what God wants them to say until they look into the faces of their people.

Again had a few simple words been like a searchlight turned upon the inner recesses of my heart. The Master continued—saying that there is no higher function than that of a minister of His Holiness the Christ, for his is the joy and duty to bring God near to the lives and hearts of men. He added that He would pray for me.

He often said that He would pray for me, and I heard Him use these words to many others. What must it have meant to the continent of America to have had the prayers of the Servant of God rising for its people! His interest in, His unbounded love for, the souls of men of every degree never flagged or failed. I remember once when I was alone with Him and the interpreter, and He had been talking for some time on deeply spiritual things, while I, silent, was filled beyond utterance with many thoughts, that He urged me to speak, saying I should tell Him all that was in my heart; that I must always be sure that my joys were His joys, and my sorrows His sorrows.

I give His words but no phrasing could convey the heavenly smile, the deep glowing eyes, the gentle tone that conveyed far more than the words.

It was about this time that I, one day, asked the Master if He would write a few words of dedication in the copy of Bahá'u'lláh's Seven Valleys, which the translator had given to me, and which I treasured much. I have before referred to the deep impression that this little book made upon me from my very first reading. Since then I had gone through it many times, and phrases, sentences, whole paragraphs had become familiar to me: outwardly familiar, that is, but the deeper meanings, the elusive, spiritual, mystic beauty of the words and the thoughts they aroused, stirred an inner depth heretofore untroubled. My heart, too, had become "fascinated by the zephyr of assurance wafted upon the garden of my innate heart from the Sheba of the Merciful." I, also, had found "all the existent beings bewildered in search of the Friend," I too was intent on attaining the "Goal of the Beloved," and "at every step I found the assistance of the Invisible surrounding me and the ardor of my search increasing." That "the steed of the Valley of Love is pain," I had faintly discerned, and with this discovery had also come a faint but blissful certainty that: "Happy is the head that is dropped in the dust in the path of His love."[10]

But, alas, not to me had been given the faintest indication of the meaning of the divine words describing the further experience of the traveler on the road "from self to God." What was the *reality* of the experience briefly hinted at as "drinking from the Cup of Abstraction"; of "hearing with divine ears and gazing on the mysteries of the Eternal One with God-like eyes"; of "stepping into the Retreat of the Friend and becoming an intimate in the Pavilion of the Beloved," and of this promise: "He (the traveler) will stretch forth the Hand of the True One from the bosom of omnipotence and show forth the mysteries of Power"? What was this divine world of the spirit from which Bahá'u'lláh sought to draw the veil? A world so vast, so beautiful, so unimaginable to our poor earth-blinded eyes and minds that even He could find no words to make it more than faintly discernible, for at times "the pen broke and the paper was torn." Or "the ink gave no result but blackness."[11]

Is it any wonder that my very soul was torn with an agonized determination to probe such depths of this mystery as my poor capacity would permit? I was "quaffing the seven seas but the thirst of my heart was not allayed." Still I was crying: "Is there yet any more? "And so, moved by the urgency of such thoughts and aspirations,

I turned to 'Abdu'l-Bahá with a certain conviction that He would understand and know that I was, at least, not one of the army of autograph seekers.

He was standing amidst a group of the friends when I approached Him but He turned to me with that courteous simplicity, which never failed, and motioned for me to speak. I handed Him the little book, and, through the interpreter, made my request, adding something of my hope to understand more and more of its hidden meanings. He smiled rather more gravely than was His wont and looked deeply into my eyes for a long moment before He signified His assent.

The next day He handed me the little volume without a word. Turning to the flyleaf I found several lines written in the beautiful copperplate Persian characters and signed by Him. It was accompanied by no English version so I hurriedly sought the interpreter and asked if he would write the translation on the opposite page.

"Very glad to do so," he answered and started to put the book in his pocket, giving no hint as to when I should recover it. But this suited my impatient soul not at all. "There are only a few lines," I suggested, "can you not write the English of it for me now? It will take but a moment." And so it was done. We found a little writing desk in a retired spot and in a few moments I had the precious book again. And this is what I read:

> O my Lord! Confirm this revered personage, that he may attain the Essential Purpose; travel in these Seven Valleys; enter the silent chamber of realities and significances, and enter the Kingdom of Mysteries.
> Verily, Thou art the Confirmer, the Helper, the Kind.
>
> (signed) 'Abdu'l-Bahá Abbas

Again He had shown an understanding of my inmost heart. What this prayer for my attainment to the "Essential Purpose" has meant to me through all these years, no words can depict. Here, indeed, "the ink gives no result but blackness."

A few days before the Sunday when 'Abdu'l-Bahá was to speak in the Brotherhood Church I was riding in the trolley car on my way to Newark, on some business connected with the building of my church edifice. As usual I had with me one of the books pertaining to the Bahá'í Faith that had come to occupy my every thought. On this occasion I was reading the volume, *Some Answered Questions,* in which 'Abdu'l-Bahá discusses some of the most vital matters pertaining to the spiritual life, mainly from the standpoint of the Christian tradition. Sitting beside me in the car was a young woman whose eyes, I noted, were straying interestedly toward the book I was reading. Obligingly I moved the book slightly toward her and so together we read those marvelously illuminating explanations for the hour-and-a-half ride to Newark. No word was spoken but I could feel that she was deeply stirred. When we reached the city and I closed the volume she said: "I think that is the most wonderful book I ever saw. Won't you tell me, please, who is the author?" So I told her of 'Abdu'l-Bahá; of His long years of exile and imprisonment for the sake of His love of truth; of His visit to America and that He was to speak in my church in Jersey City the following Sunday evening. She said: "I will surely be there." She was there. I saw her in the audience and spoke to her after the meeting. I have often wondered since whether that spark became a flame.

Perhaps it may be helpful at this time to speak of the effects which the mere reading of these divine words has produced in my own life, and the lives of many others to whom I have been privileged to introduce this new Revelation of the Eternal Logos. Over and over again I have seen hearts illumined and lives transformed by merely reading a few passages from the Hidden Words, or the Tablet to the Pope, or the Book of Certitude, or the Súratu'l-Haykal, or, in fact, from any of the books opened at random. Through these words, indeed, "flows the river of divine knowledge and bursts the fire of the consummate Wisdom of the Eternal."[12] For something like five years after meeting the Master I literally read nothing else. I crossed the continent twice during those years and carried with me a satchel filled with these books and typed copies of Tablets, which I studied constantly on the train and elsewhere. I became soaked in the "oceans of Divine utterance."[13] To this one fact alone, accompanied with constant prayer, may be ascribed whatever slight progress may have been made in the pathway of eternal life. The heavenly significances, these pearls hidden in the depths of the ocean of His verses, have opened portals to a freedom of mind and spirit such as no writings of human genius have ever bestowed. That there is a Power flowing from these words capable of bestowing a new life of faith, there has to me been abundant proof.

I remember a sincere soul of great capacity saying to me during the early days of her immersion in this ocean of revelation: "I defy anyone to study these Words with sincerity and prayerful selflessness for even such a short period as two weeks and not be assured that Bahá'u'lláh speaks with more than human tongue."

In seeking the reason for this power, I found it in Bahá'u'lláh's own explanation. In the Book of Certitude He says that in the meeting with the Manifestation, the meeting with God is attained; that after the departure from this world this meeting is assured through the meeting with His disciples, or "Family," and that after their departure this meeting is only possible through the inspired words He left to the world for the guidance and illumination of these who turn to Him.

I probed deeper, seeking practical understanding. What could this "meeting with God" mean in terms of human living? I thought to myself: When I read Emerson or Browning sympathetically and understandingly, do I not "meet" these great souls in the realm of their world? If that meeting brings to the reader such new, high, and lofty thoughts, such soaring ideals, such a change of viewpoint and such pure resolves—what must be the effect upon the aspiring soul when it "meets" the Holy Spirit of God through reverent perusal of the words of His Manifestation! I began to experience a little, at least, of the divine meaning underlying such phrases as: "ascend into the heavens of Thy knowledge"; "intoxicated with the wine of the knowledge of God"; ". . . the station of revelation and vision—before the Throne of My Grandeur."[14]

Not to the casual reader is this "meeting" vouchsafed. One must hold his breath and dive—dive deep—if the pearls of those depths are sought. But to those who, leaving all their earthly garments behind, take that selfless plunge, abandoning all else save Him, such a new and heavenly world is revealed that all verbal portrayal is beggared. A single letter of these divine words is indeed, as Bahá'u'lláh has said, "greater than the creation of heavens and earth, and which quickeneth the dead of the valley of self and desire with the spirit of faith."[15]

CHAPTER SIX

The Reality and Essence of Brotherhood. Cannot You Serve Him Once? True Brotherhood Due to the Breaths of the Holy Spirit. "O You Should Have Seen Him!"

The Prophets of God have founded the laws of divine civilization. They have been the root and fundamental source of all knowledge. They have established the principles of human brotherhood, of fraternity. . . . The spiritual brotherhood which is enkindled and established through the breaths of the Holy Spirit unites nations and removes the cause of warfare and strife. It transforms mankind into one great family and establishes the foundations of the oneness of humanity.

—'Abdu'l-Bahá,
The Promulgation of Universal Peace, p. 197

On the nineteenth of May, 1912, 'Abdu'l-Bahá spoke on brotherhood in the Brotherhood Church in Jersey City. At that time I was the unsalaried minister of that body of men and women come together spontaneously in the endeavor to foster the spirit of brotherhood and service. Only five weeks had elapsed since my first meeting with the Master. The 23rd of May, only four days later, marked the birthday of Him Who addressed us. The same day was also the sixty-eighth anniversary of the announcement by the youthful Persian Prophet, the Báb, Who declared that within nineteen years from that date there should appear "Him Whom God shall make manifest." The Báb was also one of this long line of earthly Manifestations of the Supreme One, but He said that He was not worthy to be mentioned in the Presence of Him Whose divine word was destined to sway mankind for thousands of years to come.

As I look back over the twenty-five years that have passed since that evening it stirs the imagination to consider what would have happened if the five or six hundred souls there gathered to hear speak the very son of Bahá'u'lláh, the Glory of God, to announce the coming of whom that divine youth, the Báb, had sacrificed His life; at Whose feet this son, at the age of seven years, had fallen in adoration, now stood before them. If we, brought up in the Christian tradition, could have realized that this very man Who since birth had lived with, been taught by, exiled and imprisoned with, the One for Whose coming Christ had besought us to pray and watch; if we could have recognized in Him the first citizen of that Kingdom of God on earth; and if we also had had the faith and courage to leave all and follow Him as did those sincere souls almost two thousand years ago under exactly similar conditions, consider the possible effect upon those lives and the thousands of lives they were destined to affect during the twenty-five years that have passed since then.

Also, how blind and deaf we were. No wonder that Jesus wept over Jerusalem. Blessed indeed were those in that audience, and there were some, whose eyes were open to perceive that Glory and whose ears were attuned to hear the music of that divine voice. Why this writer should have been one of those alert enough to appreciate, even a little, this supreme light, and to follow, however haltingly, those divine feet, he has never understood. It is ever the pure bounty of God. But how thankful he is that it is so. Indeed, *souls are perturbed as they make mention of Him, for minds cannot grasp Him nor hearts contain Him.*[16]

It was an impressive, even to me a thrilling sight, when the majestic figure of the Master strode up the aisle of the Brotherhood Church leading the little company of believers from various parts of the world. As memory now takes its backward look I realize how little I understood at that time the full significance of that memorable scene. Here, in a setting of Western civilization, almost two thousand years from the dawn of Christian teaching, stood One whose life and word were the very embodiment of the essence of the message of good-will to all peoples, which those nations that bear His name had seemingly forgotten. Here stood the living proof of the falsity of the assumption that East and West can never meet. Here was martyrdom for truth and love speaking lovingly and humbly to souls engrossed with self and who knew it not. Here stood the embodied spirit of holiness again uttering the eternal message of brotherhood. Here was resurrection and life again calling to those dead in the tombs of self and desire to come forth, and we recognized not His voice.

But to all such thoughts I, like most of the audience, was a stranger. Yet there was in that hall that evening an atmosphere of spiritual reality foreign to its past. It bore upon me almost unbearably and was reflected in the faces of many turned upon me as I rose to preface the talk of the Master with a few words of introduction. I can still see before me the rapt face of Lua Getsinger, one of the first American believers in the divine revelation of Bahá'u'lláh, as her unwavering gaze dwelt upon 'Abdu'l-Bahá, and the faces of many others in the audience bore similar evidence to the unaccustomed atmosphere of holiness invading their souls.

'Abdu'l-Bahá sat in the place of honor immediately behind the pulpit. Beside him sat the interpreter, who, as I spoke, translated rapidly and softly to 'Abdu'l-Bahá the essence of my words. I stood at one side of the platform so not to be in front of the Master and able to turn toward Him at times. One of my keenest remembrances of the evening is that of His attentive, smiling face while the interpreter murmured his rendering. I spoke of His forty years in the fortress of 'Akká, that indescribably filthy penal colony of the Turkish Empire; of His sixty years of exile and suffering; of the living proof He afforded that the only bondage is that of the spirit; of the evidence His presence with us that evening furnished of true spiritual brotherhood and unity. I remember particularly turning to Him apologetically as I made the personal reference to the fact that whereas other Easterners came to America exploiting its people in the name of oriental mysticism, His message bore the living imprint of self-sacrificing love. He gave while others grasped. He manifested what others mouthed. And more clearly still do I see before me that calmly smiling face, the glowing eyes, the understanding gaze with which He returned my glance.

Then 'Abdu'l-Bahá rose to speak. The interpreter stood beside Him, a little behind. "Because this is called the Church of Brotherhood I wish to speak upon the Brotherhood of Mankind."[17] As that beautifully resonant voice rang through the room, accenting with an emphasis I had never before heard, the word *brotherhood,* shame crept into my heart. Surely this man recognized connotations to that word which I, who had named the church, had never known. Who was I to stress this word? What had I ever done besides talk to prove my faith in it as a principle of life? Had I ever suffered a pang as its exponent? But this man had lived a long life in which brotherhood to all mankind had been a ruling motive. Prison nor chains; toil nor privation; hatred nor contumely had been able to turn Him from his appointed task of its exemplification, or to lessen the ardor of His proof that it was a possible goal for the race of Man. To Him, all races, colors, creeds were as one. To Him, prejudice for or against a soul because of outward wealth or poverty, sin, or virtue, was unknown. He was at every moment what in one of His divine Tablets He has told us we all must be, a "thrall of mankind."

As I write there is brought to memory a story told by Lua Getsinger, she who then sat in the audience before me. In the very early days of the knowledge of the Cause of Bahá'u'lláh in America, Mrs. Getsinger was in 'Akká having made the pilgrimage to the prison-city to see the Master. She was with Him one day when He said to her that He was too busy today to call upon a friend of His who was very ill and poor, and He wished her to go in His place. "Take him food and care for him as I have been doing," He concluded. He told her where this man was to be found and she went gladly, proud that 'Abdu'l-Bahá should trust her with this mission.

She returned quickly. "Master," she exclaimed, "surely you cannot realize to what a terrible place you sent me. I almost fainted from the awful stench, the filthy rooms, the degrading condition of that man and his house. I fled lest I contract some terrible disease."

Sadly and sternly 'Abdu'l-Bahá regarded her. "Dost thou desire to serve God," He said, "serve thy fellow man for in him dost thou see the image and likeness of God." He told her to go back to this man's house. If it is filthy she should clean it; if this brother of yours is dirty, bathe him; if he is hungry, feed him. Do not return until this is done. Many times had He done this for him and cannot she serve him once?

This was He who was speaking in my Church of Brotherhood.

He spoke of the contrast between physical and spiritual brotherhood, pointing out that the latter was the only real and lasting relationship. "This divine fellowship," He said, "owes its existence to the breaths of the Holy Spirit. Spiritual brotherhood is like the light while the souls of mankind are as lanterns. These incandescent lamps," pointing to the electric lights illuminating the hall, "are many but the light is one." He spoke of the influence Bahá'u'lláh exerted in bringing amity and friendship into some of the warring and antagonistic peoples and religions of the Orient.[18]

"He breathed such a spirit into those countries," He said, "that various peoples and warring tribes were blended into unity. Their bestowals and susceptibilities; their purposes and desires became one to such a degree that they sacrificed themselves for one another, forfeiting name, possessions and comfort. This is eternal, spiritual fellowship, heavenly and divine brotherhood which defies dissolution."[19]

This was, indeed, a new type of brotherhood. Not a fraternal partnership, so to speak, which had as its objective a mutual sharing of the good things of the world more easily attained and more safely held by reason of this partnership. But rather a rebirth of men through a new baptism of the Holy Spirit, who by this rebirth found themselves actually conscious of a heavenly, spiritual, divine kinship that transcended any earthly relationship as the music of the spheres transcended earth's discordance.

And as I gazed at the Master as I faced Him from the audience, it was not so difficult to imagine a world transformed by the spirit of divine brotherhood. For He Himself was that spirit incarnate. His flowing 'abá, His creamlike fez, His silvery hair and beard, all set Him apart from the Westerners to whom He spake. But His smile, which seemed to embrace us with an overflowing comradeship; His eyes, which flashed about the room as if seeking out each individual; His gestures, which combined such authority and humility, such wisdom and humor; all conveyed to me, at least, a true human brotherhood, which could never be content with plenty while the least of these little ones had less than enough, and yet still less content until all had that divine plenty only to be bestowed through the breaths of the Holy Spirit, that is, by contact with the Manifestation of God. He closed with the following words, as recorded in the first volume of *The Promulgation of Universal Peace:*

Trust in the favor of God. Look not at your own capacities, for the divine bestowals can transform a drop into an ocean; it can make a tiny seed a lofty tree. Verily divine bestowals are like the sea and we are like the fishes in that sea. The fishes must not look at themselves. They must behold the ocean which is vast and wonderful. Provision for the sustenance of all is in this ocean, therefore the divine bounties encompass all and love eternal shines upon all.[20]

It was one of the briefest of 'Abdu'l-Bahá's public talks. The latter part, as recorded in *The Promulgation of Universal Peace,* was in answer to a question from the audience, which was a departure from the usual custom. I had requested of the Master that He speak rather longer than was His wont as I had the universal obsession that the worth of an address was in proportion to its length. That He spoke so briefly was undoubtedly with the endeavor to illustrate to me that a very few words, inspired by the Holy Spirit and aglow with wisdom celestial, were vastly more powerful than all the volumes of manmade sermons ever printed.

That I should have had the temerity to make such a request of Him again illustrates how far removed I still was from recognition of His station; nay from any true understanding of spiritual reality. I, even now, only dimly realize it and I suspect that the vast majority of my fellowmen share with me this abysmal ignorance. Bahá'u'lláh has said that compared to the wonders and glories of the spiritual universe the material universe is comparable to "the black of the eye of a dead ant."[21] And I had requested this man, to Whom that universe of the spirit was as an open book, to make His talk of a length suitable to my own desires. And He had in fifteen minutes said more, and shown forth more, and loved more of the true brotherhood, the heavenly and divine brotherhood, which could transform this world into a paradise, than I had ever dreamed.

How blind and deaf we are! And what a fearful price the world is paying for this imperviousness to that "Light which lighteth every man who cometh into the world!"

On May 24, five days after He spoke in the Brotherhood Church, 'Abdu'l-Bahá addressed the assembled ministers at the annual May Meeting of the Unitarian Fellowship in Boston. Present

were the representatives of the Unitarian Faith in America, an intellectual group holding, probably, the most "advanced" opinions
in religious thought in the country. Yet He spoke to deaf ears. "A
very interesting old gentleman," several remarked to me afterwards, "but he told us nothing new."

This was typical of most of the audiences He addressed. Truly,
"having ears we heard not." I would suggest that the reader of
these words again peruse that Boston address as found in the first
volume of *The Promulgation of Universal Peace,* p. 138,* as I have
just done, and determine for himself whether anything "new" is
to be found there. "The divine Prophets have revealed and founded religion," 'Abdu'l-Bahá said. This may not be new in the sense
that this teaching had never been formulated, but to this Boston
audience, which had unanimously, not to say enthusiastically, re-
jected all belief in a revealed religion it was fundamentally new
because the speaker was actually the physical son of the latest of
these divine Prophets Who had lived and taught, suffered and
died, during the lifetime of some of His listeners. 'Abdu'l-Bahá's
whole address was directed to calling attention to the fact that
the tree of religion grows old and withers like any tree, and that
unless a new tree is planted from the seed of the old, true religion
perishes from the earth. His audience was composed of men and
women whose lives were dedicated to an attempt to revive this
withered and dying tree, and they were watering it, not with the
"water of certitude," which flows only from the lips of the divine
Revelator Himself, but with manmade theories and theologies,
which, as their own experience should have taught them, they are
forced to renounce almost as soon as accepted. "Nothing new!"
Had they known how this news was destined to revolutionize the
world of thought and action; how it was to arouse in mankind a
new passion for unity and brotherhood; how it was destined to be

---

* See 'Abdu'l-Bahá, *The Promulgation of Universal Peace.* Wilmette, IL: Bahá'í
Publishing Trust, 2007 [pp. 193–98].

the moving spirit behind all efforts toward the abolition of war, poverty, disease, and crime; how men's hearts would be aroused to a new life by the breaths of its Holy Spirit; how all human life would take on a new meaning, significance, and power; His hearers would have transcribed His divine words "with a pen of diamond on a page of gold."[22]

To me, 'Abdu'l-Bahá's talk in the Brotherhood Church and the address before the Unitarian Conference in Boston marked a new phase in my spiritual journey from self to God. I had heard several of His public addresses before but never had I been near enough to Him to mark closely His demeanor. For it was not only His words, not nearly so much His accents and voice which now impressed me. There lay in His eyes a living flame, which seemed to ignite a smoldering spark within me. Perhaps I can express my meaning best by relating an incident.

At one of the meetings at the home of the friends to whom I have often referred, where the Master spent much of His time in New York, there was present a lady who was not, and never became an avowed believer. But her heart was pure. She loved Christ and strove to follow His divine teachings. The large double rooms were filled with the friends and attracted souls. A lane had been left open stretching the full length of both rooms, and, as the Master spoke, He strode up and down the rooms while the interpreter stood near me translating fluently. This lady sat enthralled. When 'Abdu'l-Bahá came striding toward us with that indescribable grace and majesty, His hands gesturing rhythmically with an upward, inspiring significance, which I have seen in no other speaker, and His eyes glowing with an inner light illumining every feature, she was overcome with emotion.

Several months afterwards, I was talking with a close friend of this soul and she asked me about 'Abdu'l-Bahá, Whom she had never seen. "He must be a very wonderful man from what . . . says," she remarked, mentioning the name of the woman, "she tried to tell me about Him and could hardly speak for tears. I said to her:

'Why, my dear, what was there so wonderful about this man?' All she could say was: "Oh, you should have *seen* Him. You should have *seen* Him!"

Indeed to have seen Him was enough providing that the spark ignited in the soul was fanned to flame by meditation and selfless prayer. Never can I be thankful enough that I became ignited with this flame. It was about this time, seven weeks after meeting 'Abdu'l-Bahá, that I began to say a little hymn to myself: "If every drop of my blood had a million tongues and every tongue sang praises throughout eternity, sufficient thanksgiving could not be uttered."

CHAPTER SEVEN

MARRIAGE UNDER THE WORLD ORDER OF BAHÁ'U'LLÁH:
AN ETERNAL BOND. THE WEDDING.
THE NEED FOR REFORMATION OF LAWS
PERTAINING TO DIVORCE.
THE LAWS OF BAHÁ'U'LLÁH. FOUR KINDS OF LOVE.
THE CHILDREN OF THE NEW DAY.

> *It is, therefore, evident that in the world of human-*
> *ity the greatest king and sovereign is love. If love were*
> *extinguished, the power of attraction dispelled, the*
> *affinity of human hearts destroyed, the phenomena of*
> *human life would disappear.*
>
> —'Abdu'l-Bahá,
> *The Promulgation of Universal Peace,* p. 357

In tracing the development of the institution of marriage it is interesting to note that the progressive steps, from the promiscuity of the
earliest history of mankind to the more or less monogamous ordi-
nance now in vogue in most civilized countries, have been in direct
ratio to the ethical and spiritual development of the race. Moreover
this development has paralleled the appearance and teachings of
the great Prophets and Messengers of God to mankind.

What little is known of the matrimonial relations and customs
of the various peoples before the coming of Moses, Buddha, Jesus,

and Muhammad, indicates much looser and more unethical relations than obtained after Their teaching.

One might reasonably expect, therefore, that the revelation of Bahá'u'lláh and its exemplification by 'Abdu'l-Bahá, in dealing with this subject, would lay down laws and prescribe regulations founded upon eternal spiritual principles and adapted to the needs of a world civilization far in advance of any hitherto practiced.

For the teachings of Bahá'u'lláh deal primarily with the reality of man, and his station as an immortal and eternal being in an infinite universe governed and supported by immutable laws based upon righteousness and truth.

Marriage, then, under the Bahá'í regime, is an eternal bond. It allows for only one real marriage, and this union continues throughout all the worlds of God.

This assumption makes necessary an entirely new regulation of both marriage and divorce. For, since man is still in the age of immaturity, and is still influenced by desire and passion, many mistakes will be made in the selection of a mate, and these mistakes must be rectified as quickly and as simply as possible.

For two souls to live together under an enforced union in which harmony, cooperation, happiness, and true eternal love have become impossible, is a defiance of a basic law in the Bahá'í revelation—the law of unity. It is not only desirable but allowable that such false union be dissolved. This necessity will probably be extremely rare as the race comes more and more under the influence of the whole range of the divine teachings. For once man realizes the supreme joy of true physical and spiritual union, he will be content with nothing less. Moreover, Bahá'u'lláh has framed such safeguarding laws, and 'Abdu'l-Bahá has explained them so fully, that public opinion will tend more and more to enforce their obedience as experience proves their efficacy in securing and perpetuating human happiness.

When 'Abdu'l-Bahá was in this country in 1912 He took occasion more than once to emphasize the sacredness of the marriage bond, and to illustrate by precept and example the attitude incumbent upon the Bahá'ís in its observance.

The most notable of these occasions was the wedding ceremony on July 17, 1912 in which Harlan Ober and Grace Robarts were united by 'Abdu'l-Bahá Himself in accordance with the law of Bahá'u'lláh.

'Abdu'l-Bahá suggested that I should assist Him by performing the necessary legal ceremony in order "that all should be done in accordance with the law of the land."

It is not an easy task to present to minds obsessed with the conception of this world and its affairs as complete in itself rather than as an anteroom to a larger, freer life, a scene in which the dominant note was *eternity;* the very atmosphere charged with an expansive freedom and tranquility.

As my eyes took in that long, beautifully furnished room, speaking of all that related to our modern culture, yet holding within its walls representatives of Paris; Berlin; London; Tehran and Ghom, Persia; Bombay, India; Bákú, Russia; and Haifa, Palestine; quite a number of representatives of the black race, and about one hundred of my own countrymen, a conviction was borne upon me that I was taking part in a truly epoch-making event.

For here was, to all intents and purposes, a gathering of representatives of the whole world, and of every degree of poverty and affluence; of culture and its lack; of every range of spiritual capacity.

Here indeed the East and West were gathered together to witness a prefigurement, a symbol, a prognosis of a fundamental detail of the coming social order under the World Plan of Bahá'u'lláh, the Kingdom of God upon earth.

Dominating the scene was the white-robed figure of the Master. From the age of seven He has been addressed and spoken of by this title. Bahá'u'lláh Himself indicated His wish that so He should be addressed.

His right to the title did not rest upon any assumption by Himself of authority or precedence. His whole bearing was ever that of humility and gentle deference. Yet in every home He entered He was the host, in every gathering the center, in every discussion the arbiter, to every problem the answer.

Nor was it so because He wished or willed it so to be. On the contrary, when He was asked to act as honorary chairman of the New York Bahá'í Assembly (one of the 72 incipient Houses of Justice in this country, which, in the future will form the units of community government under the Plan of Bahá'u'lláh), He calmly and decisively replied that "'Abdu'l-Bahá is a servant."

Nevertheless one could not be in His Presence more than a few moments without realizing that His every act, tone, gesture, word was so imbued with wisdom, courage, and tranquil certitude, combined with such humble consideration of His interlocutor, that conclusive truth was conveyed to every beholder and listener. As 'Abdu'l-Bahá has said, referring to Bahá'u'lláh when confronting His deniers and opposers, "How can darkness assert itself in the Presence of Light? Can a fly attack an eagle? Or the shadow defy the sun?"

And so, in this gathering of souls believing in a new era of human consciousness; a new epoch in which that consciousness should merge into the divine, we looked to Him as to the Master of our destinies, as the one leader Who, in this time of ancient superstitions and modern follies, knew the way out of the human labyrinth into the glorious freedom of the children of God.

I sat very near Him, and, naturally, my every faculty, eye, ear, mind, and heart, were centered upon that radiant personality. Nor was I alone in this. There was but one worthy of attention when He was present; but one wholly satisfying.

After the simple wedding ceremony, as the bride and groom had resumed their seats, 'Abdu'l-Bahá rose. His cream-colored 'abá fell in graceful folds to His feet. Upon His head He wore a tarboosh, or fez, of the same color, beneath which His long white hair fell almost to His shoulders. Most impressive of all His impressive aspects were His eyes. Blue they were but so changing with

His mood! Now gentle and appealing; now commanding; now flashing with hidden fires; now holding a deep, tranquil, lambent repose as though gazing upon scenes of glory far removed.

His brow above those wide-set eyes was like an ivory dome. His neatly clipped beard, snowy white, touched His breast, but around His mouth no straggling hairs obscured the mobile lips.

He spoke through an interpreter, as was His custom, not so much because He could not use English, as that it was wise to guard against possible misquotation. Every word He uttered while in America was transcribed as it fell from His lips by a Persian secretary, in that language, and also by an American stenographer as the interpreter followed. So that in future ages, when the thousands of writings and addresses of Bahá'u'lláh and 'Abdu'l-Bahá are translated and codified, there may never be any question as to the actual words and their connotation.

He swept the room with a glance at once enfolding and abstracted. He raised His hands, palm upwards, level with His waist, His eyes closed, and He chanted a prayer for the souls united by Him and by me. By Him that morning according to the laws of the New World Order in which the spirit of man is to be trained to function harmoniously with its brief material environment; by me this evening as the representative of the passing regime in which ancient superstitions and outworn shibboleths often tinge the most sacred observances, yet which, being customary, are to be observed "lest offense be given to any soul."

This prayer of 'Abdu'l-Bahá, chanted in tones to me unequalled in all experience, mellifluous (honey-like), is the nearest descriptive word, but how inadequate, is the keenest of all my memories of that evening.

In spite of the fact that the language was Persian, and so, of course, unfamiliar to me, the impression I received was that of understanding.

So vivid was this that the interpreter's translation came as a shock. What need to translate language addressed to the spirit? A flash of comprehension came to me. Perhaps here was the explanation of the incident recorded of that far-off Day of Pentecost when each listener to the words of the disciples heard his own tongue.

There is a story told of an illiterate miner who made a long journey on foot to meet 'Abdu'l-Bahá when He was in San Francisco, which further illustrates the same spiritual phenomenon. This man, though uneducated, had great spiritual capacity. He attended a meeting at which 'Abdu'l-Bahá spoke. He seemed enthralled as the measured, bell-like tones fell from the Master's lips. When the interpreter took up the passage in English this miner started as if awakening. "Why does that man interrupt?" he whispered. Then again 'Abdu'l-Bahá spoke, and again the visitor was lost in attention. Again the interpreter translated as the speaker paused. At this the miner's indignation was aroused. "Why do they let that man interrupt? He should be put out."

"He is the official interpreter," one sitting beside him explained. "He translates the Persian into English."

"Was He speaking in Persian?" was the naive answer, "Why, anyone could understand that."

As for me: my heart was certainly moved far more by the chanting Voice and the flowing, musical periods, than by the interpreter's version of the wedding prayer, beautiful as it is.

Glory be unto Thee, O my God! Verily, this Thy servant and this Thy maidservant have gathered under the shadow of Thy mercy and they are united through Thy favor and generosity. O Lord! Assist them in this Thy world and Thy kingdom and destine for them every good through Thy bounty and grace. O Lord! Confirm them in Thy servitude and assist them in Thy service. Suffer them to become the signs of Thy Name in Thy world and protect them through Thy bestowals which are inexhaustible in this world and the world to come. O Lord! They are supplicating the kingdom of Thy mercifulness and invoking the realm of Thy singleness. Verily, they are married in obedience to Thy command. Cause them to become the signs of harmony and unity until the end of time. Verily, Thou art the Omnipotent, the Omnipresent and the Almighty![23]

As intimated (p. 72), marriage under the World Order of Bahá'u'lláh is based upon a far nobler conception of man's destiny than ever before. This is because under the 1900 years of Christian teaching the spiritual capacity of the race has developed to a point where such conception of man's station is at least comprehensible.

The object of the coming of the Manifestations of God is none other than the raising of man's consciousness to a higher level. This is one of the meanings of "Heaven" as used by the prophets of God.[24] It is that state of consciousness to which the teachings of the eternal Christ spirit, no matter under what name He rises upon the horizon of history, exalts the spirit of the true believer.

It is essential, then, that under each new dispensation the eternal principles, reiterated by each Messenger of God, should be so clarified and explained that they will apply effectively to the problems of the new day. So when Jesus appeared He abrogated the Mosaic Law regarding divorce, which, while perfectly adapted to the nomadic life of the Hebrews and to their background of centuries of slavery under Egypt, had become subject to such abuse under the changed conditions of the Roman environment, and the sacerdotalism of the Pharisee and priest, as to become a mockery.

It is plain that at this time the same observance of the letter of Christ's teachings on this subject prevails, and total neglect of the spirit. In America, supposedly a Christian social order, the marriage bond is regarded with less sacredness than in any other country in the world. In 1930, the latest census, there was one divorce to every six marriages. And who can number the infringements of the wedding vow; the hatreds in the home; the broken family circles that never reached the divorce court? Plainly this is an intolerable condition. If it were to continue unchecked, it might well result in a complete breaking down of family life and the utter destruction of the institution of marriage. Indeed this social breakdown has already begun in Russia, and is threatened in one or two other countries. And what is becoming known as "free love" and "companionate marriage" is obtaining recognition in some of our own educational institutions and actually taught as the only solution of the spreading problem.

This problem is so momentous, its solution so fraught with danger or safety to the destinies of the race, that this servant of the Glory of God has gathered all the available information possible on the subject and presents the actual wording of Bahá'u'lláh and 'Abdu'l-Bahá, in order that the reader may judge for himself whether, if and when these divine laws become operative, a happier social order would result.

In the first place it must constantly be borne in mind that Bahá'u'lláh envisages a *world* unity; a *world* order. It assumes, moreover, the close association of man with God, and presumes the assistance of the supreme world, the Holy Spirit, in the establishment of this Order.

Thus, in the conception of the Kingdom of God on earth, Bahá'u'lláh sees as accomplished the unity of all races and peoples; the abolition of all prejudice; an inherent and passionate love for truth, no matter from what source it comes; and the spread of basic education in these laws to all peoples.

Thus He has generalized broadly, encompassing the problems of East and West, of North and South, leaving to the International House of Justice* the application of these principles as special and individual problems arise.

---

* The Universal House of Justice—ordained in the writings of Bahá'u'lláh, elucidated upon in the writings of 'Abdu'l-Bahá and Shoghi Effendi, and established in 1963—is the supreme institution, and the international governing body, of the Bahá'í Faith.

If the reader will bear this in mind, and make every effort to disabuse himself of the very natural prejudices he may have entertained, it will be much easier for him to appreciate the wisdom of Bahá'u'lláh's plan for a New World Order.

This is not an easy task to set oneself, for man naturally tends to accept as fixed the conventions and usages obtaining at that moment of history in which he has happened to appear upon the planet. But to do this is to disregard all the records of the past, which indicate most clearly the inevitable mutation or abolition of all human institutions, and the general tendency, throughout the ages, to simplify, purify, and ennoble them. The destiny of the race is very high, and even the laws of Bahá'u'lláh are not proposed as final. The next thousand or ten thousand years will witness still further advances by mankind along the path to the divine perfection to which all the Prophets of God have summoned him. *"Ye must be perfect, even as your Father in Heaven is perfect."*

At this stage in the development of the race, the laws promulgated by Bahá'u'lláh assuredly seem to meet most adequately the needs of men taken as a whole. To those who study the writings of Bahá'u'lláh, paying due attention to the claim of majestic authority involved, these sublime words calling man to participate in a social order far higher than that ever envisaged in the past, can hardly fail to stimulate a dawning hope, revive a failing courage, and again set ablaze the fire of the love of God in cooling hearts.

Bearing all this in mind let us endeavor to approach the subject of marriage relations, as taught by Bahá'u'lláh, with the thoughtful consideration, if not reverence, due any teacher Who, for the sake of the Message which He was convinced He bore for men, suffering every indignity, humiliation and torture which the ingenuity of two cruel rulers and their peoples, the Sháh of Persia and the Sultan of Turkey, could over a period of forty years, inflict upon Him.

That the reader may receive an idea of the claim put forth by Bahá'u'lláh regarding the Source of His authority and the objectives toward which He urges humanity, the following paragraph is quoted from His writings lately translated by His great-grandson, Shoghi Effendi, the first Guardian of the Bahá'í Faith:*

> The first duty prescribed by God for His servants is the recognition of Him Who is the Dayspring of His Revelation and the Fountain of His Laws, Who representeth the Godhead in both the Kingdom of His Cause and the world of creation. . . .
>
> They whom God hath endued with insight will readily recognize that the precepts laid down by God constitute the highest means for the maintenance of order in the world and the security of its peoples. He that turneth away from them is accounted among the abject and foolish. We verily have commanded you to refuse the dictates of your evil passions and corrupt desires, and not to transgress the bounds which the Pen of the Most High hath fixed, for these are the breath of life unto all created beings. The seas of Divine Wisdom and divine utterance have risen under the breath of the breeze of the All-Merciful. Hasten to drink your fill, O men of understanding.[25]

Regarding marriage, the following is a summary of the ordinances prescribed by the "Pen of the Most High (Bahá'u'lláh)" for the guidance of the race for the coming thousand or thousands of years. Again the reader's attention should be called to the fact that the Lawgiver envisages, not one nation or religion or group, but the whole world.

Bahá'u'lláh enjoined marriage upon all, and monogamy is assumed as the only means of content(ment) and happiness. He condemned the attitude of certain religious groups in various creedal

---

* While provisions were made in the Will and Testament of 'Abdu'l-Bahá for a hereditary successorship within the institution of the Guardianship, Shoghi Effendi left no heir and named no successor prior to his passing in 1957, and was therefore the only Guardian of the Bahá'í Faith.

systems that forbade marriage to their priesthood. "Enter into wed-lock," He said, "that ye may bring forth one who will make mention of Me amid My servants."[26]

He directed that marriage should depend first upon the consent of both parties concerned and also upon the consent of the parents of both, as He desires "love, unity and harmony" to exist between all the servants of God, "lest enmity and rancor should arise amongst them."[27]

A dowry is recommended, paid by the man to the woman, and He designates the amount, which is quite small.* The object, evidently being to avoid the sense of absolute dependence of the wife upon the husband. This is especially important in oriental countries.

In case of disagreement between man and wife, if any agitation or aversion arise, he must not divorce her, but be patient one year, that "perhaps the fragrance of love may emanate from them." If, however, at the expiration of that time "no fragrance of love be diffused," divorce is allowed.

'Abdu'l-Bahá, in a Tablet to the Bahá'ís of America, wrote as follows:

"The friends (Bahá'ís) must strictly refrain from divorce unless something arises which compels them to separate because of their aversion for each other; in that case, with the knowledge of the Spiritual Assembly, they may decide to separate. They must then be patient and wait one complete year. If during this year

---

* The law regarding the payment of a dowry as stipulated in the Kitáb-i-Aqdas has little in common with traditional practices found in various cultures, and is intended as a symbolic act. As with many laws established by Bahá'u'lláh in the Kitáb-i-Aqdas, this one is not yet universally applied. The appropriate time for the application of this law is left to the discretion of the Universal House of Justice—the international governing body of the Bahá'í Faith. See Bahá'u'lláh, *The Kitáb-i-Aqdas*. Wilmette, IL: Bahá'í Publishing Trust, 1993. [¶66; p. 208, note 93.]

harmony is not reestablished between them, then their divorce may be realized. . . . The foundation of the Kingdom of God is based upon harmony and love, oneness, relationship and union, not upon differences, especially between husband and wife. If one of these two become the cause of divorce, that one will unquestionably fall into great difficulties, will become the victim of formidable calamities and experience deep remorse."[28]

Bahá'u'lláh exhorts men not to follow their material self, for it is an instigator to transgression and foul actions, but rather to follow the Ruler of all things Who commandeth them to practice virtue and righteousness. It is such constant references to a supreme law, coupled with a sympathetic consideration of human weakness, which makes the study of His writings so enthralling. One looks in vain into the statute books of past and present for any such atmosphere of commingled authority and love. The Mosaic Law conveys no hint of such. It is as if the Sermon on the Mount were reduced to a code and laid upon men with gentle hands. In this fact lies the assurance not only of its divine origin but of its ultimate acceptance by the world. For when the heart of man is appealed to as well as his reason, he is perforce enlisted on the side of the Law proposed. As an illustration of this appeal, Bahá'u'lláh urges upon the husband, when undertaking an extended absence from his wife, to acquaint her with particulars of his movements and an appointed time for his return. "If he return by the promised time, he will have obeyed the bidding of his Lord and shall be numbered by the Pen of His behest among the righteous." If a real excuse prevents his return he must inform his wife and strive to return. If this is not done she must wait nine months, at the expiration of which time she is free to choose another husband. "but should she wait longer, God, verily, loveth those women and men who show forth patience. . . . If, during the period of her waiting, word should reach her from her husband, she should choose the course that is praiseworthy. He, of a truth, desireth that His servants and His handmaids should be at peace with one another; . . ."*[29]

Picture the courts of the future where such an atmosphere obtains. If the reader is inclined to doubt that such should ever be possible, far be it from me to cast aspersions. None could possibly be a greater doubter than I. Yet I have come to see in the divine words of Bahá'u'lláh, not only beauty and wisdom, but an indwelling potency to sway the human heart and will. The fact that several millions of the world's peoples have already subscribed to His teachings and laws, often at the cost of property and life, may be accounted as, at least, some slight reason to hope that at some not far distant day an influential minority of sane men will accept and put in practice these divine precepts.

Regarding the provision concerning the consent of the parents of both parties to the marriage, 'Abdu'l-Bahá once wrote to an inquirer that this consent was to be obtained *after* a mutual satisfactory arrangement had been arrived at by the contracting parties. Before that the parents had no right of interference. This abrogates the practice usual in the Orient by which the parents arrange the marriage, often without the consent or wish of the persons most interested. He further says that as a result of these provisions, the strained relations between relatives-in-law, which have become proverbial in Christian and Muhammadan countries, are almost unknown among the Bahá'ís, and divorce is also a rare occurrence.[30]

Many have been the utterances and writings of 'Abdu'l-Bahá on this subject. Following are some of the most important:

---

* The apparent intention of this law is to establish the conditions under which it may be assumed that a wife has been abandoned by her husband so as to allow her to remarry without divorce or confirmation of her husband's death. As with many laws established by Bahá'u'lláh in the Kitáb-i-Aqdas, this one is not yet universally applied. The appropriate time for the application of this law is left to the discretion of the Universal House of Justice—the international governing body of the Bahá'í Faith. See Bahá'u'lláh, *The Kitáb-i-Aqdas*. Wilmette, IL: Bahá'í Publishing Trust, 1993. [¶67; p. 210, notes 96–98.]

In this most Merciful Age the ignorant prejudices are entirely removed. The Bahá'í engagement is the perfect communication and the entire consent of both parties. However, they must show forth the utmost attention and become informed of one another's character, and the firm covenant between them must become an eternal bond, and their intention must be everlasting affinity, friendship, unity and life. The bridegroom must, before the bridesmen and few others, say: "Verily, we are content with the Will of God." And the bride must rejoin: "Verily, we are satisfied with the desire of God." This is Bahá'í matrimony.[31]

Regarding the question of matrimony: know that the command of marriage is eternal. It will never be changed or altered. This is a Divine Creation and there is not the slightest possibility that change or alteration shall affect this Divine Creation (marriage).[32]

Among the majority of the people marriage consists of physical relationship and this union and relationship is temporary for at the end physical separation is destined and ordained. But the marriage of the people of Bahá must consist of both physical and spiritual relationship for both of them are intoxicated with the wine of one cup, are attracted by one Peerless Countenance, are quickened with one Life and are illumined with one Light. This is the spiritual relationship and everlasting union. Likewise in the physical world they are bound together with strong and unbreakable ties.

When relationship, union and concord exist between the two from a physical and spiritual standpoint, that is the real union, therefore everlasting. But if the union is merely from the physical point of view, unquestionably it is temporal and at the end separation is inevitable.

Consequently when the people of Bahá desire to enter the sacred union of marriage, eternal connection and ideal relationship, spiritual and physical association of thoughts and conceptions of life must exist between them, so that in all the grades of existence and all the worlds of God this union may continue forever and ever for this real union is a splendor of the light of the love of God.

Likewise if the souls become real believers they will find themselves ushered into this exalted state of relationship, becoming the manifestors of the love of the Merciful and exhilarated with the cup of the love of God. Undoubtedly that union and relationship is eternal.

The souls who sacrifice self, become detached from the imperfections of the realm of man and free from the shackles of this ephemeral world, assuredly the splendors of the rays of divine union shall shine in their hearts and in the eternal paradise they shall find ideal relationship, union and happiness.

(Signed) 'Abdu'l-Bahá Abbas[33]

In the first two of the above selections it will be noted that the emphasis is upon the eternality of the true marriage union. In the third quotation, a careful reading will disclose the three ways in which this unending union may be achieved, (a) When two souls on the altars of whose hearts burns the fire of the love of God, find that light reflected in each other and that flame, commingled, becomes one fire. (b) When two souls having become united in physical union, afterward become illumined by the Eternal Love, that union also becomes eternal. 'Abdu'l-Bahá once wrote concerning a believer who had married a non-believer, or was about to marry: "This marriage is permissible, but Miss——must exert herself day and night so that she may guide her husband. She must not rest until she makes him her spiritual as well as physical partner in life."[34]

(c) The last paragraph relates to those souls who never in this world find their true spiritual mate, and remain deprived throughout this transitory life of that great joy. To such He [essentially] says: If you become detached from this ephemeral world and the imperfections of the realms of man, "assuredly the splendors of the rays of divine union shall shine" in your heart and you "shall find ideal relationship, union and happiness."

Speaking of the reality of love, 'Abdu'l-Bahá said:

There are four kinds of love. The first is the love that flows from God to man; it consists of the inexhaustible graces, the Divine effulgence and heavenly illumination. Through this love the world of being receives life. Through this love man is endowed with physical existence, until, through the breath of the Holy Spirit—this same love—he receives eternal life and becomes the image of the Living God. This love is the origin of all the love in the world of creation.

The second is the love that flows from man to God. This is faith, attraction to the Divine, enkindlement, progress, entrance into the Kingdom of God, receiving the Bounties of God, illumination with the lights of the Kingdom. This love is the origin of all philanthropy; this love causes the hearts of men to reflect the rays of the Sun of Reality.

The third is the love of God towards the Self or Identity of God. This is the transfiguration of His Beauty, the reflection of Himself in the mirror of His Creation. This is the reality of love, the Ancient Love, the Eternal Love. Through one ray of this Love all other love exists.

The fourth is the love of man for man. The love which exists between the hearts of believers is prompted by the ideal of the unity of spirits. This love is attained through the knowledge of God, so that men see the Divine Love reflected in the heart. Each sees in the other the Beauty of God reflected in the soul, and finding this point of similarity, they are attracted to one another in love. This love will make all men the waves of one sea, this love will make them all the stars of one heaven and the fruits of one tree. This love will bring the realization of true accord, the foundation of real unity.

But the love which sometimes exists between friends is not (true) love, because it is subject to transmutation; this is merely fascination. As the breeze blows, the slender trees yield. If the wind is in the East the tree leans to the West, and if the wind turns to the West the tree leans to the East. This kind of love is originated by the accidental conditions of life. This is not love, it is merely acquaintanceship; it is subject to change.[35]

It seems impossible to read these divine words without an inner conviction growing in the heart that man, in this dispensation, is being ushered into a new and hitherto unrealized world: the world of reality; the world of the spirit. No imagination can compass the world of man, the coming social order, when it becomes impregnated with this spirit, when it becomes illumined, as it surely will, by this supreme Sun.

And when we have seen in the very life of 'Abdu'l-Bahá, this light manifested, when before our eyes we have witnessed the power and beauty of such ideals fully expressed, and are told in words of matchless beauty and wisdom that such a life may be approximated by all who submit themselves to the rays of the supreme love, how the heart is stirred to realize this experience, and the will summoned to assist, to one's fullest capacity, in bringing about this Kingdom of love upon the earth!

'Abdu'l-Bahá's many references to the *children* of the New Day invite the mind to a most enthralling consideration. His allusions to such children, especially when born of such heavenly union as already described, are many and beautiful. Taken in connection with the foregoing excerpts on marriage, and its eternal bond, they give a faint indication of what human society may be when the World Order of Bahá'u'lláh is established. Space can be given to only two or three citations.

These children are neither Oriental nor Occidental, neither Asiatic nor American, neither European nor African, but they are of the Kingdom; their native home is heaven and their resort is the Kingdom of Abhá.[36]

The newly born babe of that Day excels the wisest and most venerable men of this time, and the lowliest and most unlearned of that period shall surpass in understanding the most erudite and accomplished divines of this age.

The Báb to His disciples[37]

As to thy question concerning training children: It is incumbent upon thee to nurture them from the breast of the love of God, to urge them towards spiritual matters, to turn unto God and to acquire good manners, best characteristics and praiseworthy virtues and qualities in the world of humanity, and to study sciences with the utmost diligence; so that they may become spiritual, heavenly and attracted to the fragrances of sanctity from their childhood and be reared in a religious, spiritual and heavenly training.[38]

A CHILD'S PRAYER

O My Lord! O my Lord!

I am a child of tender years. Nourish me from the breast of Thy mercy, train me in the bosom of Thy love, educate me in the school of Thy guidance and develop me under the shadow of Thy bounty. Deliver me from darkness, make me a brilliant light; free me from unhappiness, make me a flower of the rose garden; suffer me to become a servant of Thy threshold and confer upon me the disposition and nature of the righteous; make me a cause of bounty to the human world, and crown my head with the diadem of eternal life.

Verily, Thou art the Powerful, the Mighty, the Seer, the Hearer.[39]

CHAPTER EIGHT

In Dublin, N. H. with 'Abdu'l-Bahá.
"The Most Perfect Gentleman I Have Ever Known."
The Master Teacher. The Spiritual Warrior.
A Fable. "It Behooves You to Manifest Light."
The Gift. The First Tablet.

*We have come here for work and Service, not for
enjoyment of air and scenery.*
—'Abdu'l-Bahá in Dublin, N. H.

In August of that year in which a new world opened, an invitation
came to me to be the guest of 'Abdu'l-Bahá in Dublin, N. H.

One of the Washington friends, at whose home in that city
'Abdu'l-Bahá had visited and spoken several times, had offered
Him the use of a large farmhouse on her lovely estate in Dublin.
As this house, however, was pretty well filled with the large party
of Persian and American friends who accompanied Him, He had
taken a room in the Dublin Inn and it was there He entertained
me, over the weekend of August 9, 1912.

Dublin is a beautiful mountain summer resort where gathers
each year a colony of wealthy intellectuals from Washington, D. C.
and from various large centers. 'Abdu'l-Bahá's stay in that place
for a period of three weeks offers another evidence of His unique
power of adaptation to every environment; His dominant humil-

ity in every group, which, while seeming to follow He really led; and His manifest, all-embracing knowledge.

Picture, if you can, this Oriental, fresh from more than fifty years of exile and prison-life, suddenly placed in an environment representing the proudest culture of the Western world. Nothing in His life, one would reasonably presume, had offered a preparation for such a contact. Not to His youth had been given years of academic and scholastic training. Not to His young manhood had been supplied those subtle associations during His formative years. Not upon His advancing age had been bestowed the comforts and leisure, which invite the mind's expanse.

Quite the contrary, as I have endeavored to portray, His life had been a constant submission to every form of hardship and deprivation, when considered from a material standpoint alone. Dungeons and chains had been His lot. Torture not seldom; confinement in the stocks, or any indignity that heartless jailers might design, His portion. The Bible and the Koran, His only books.

How, then, can it be explained that in this environment He not only mingled with these highest products of wealth and culture with no slightest embarrassment to them or to Him, but He literally outshone them in their chosen field.

No matter what subject was brought up He was perfectly at home in its discussion, yet always with an undercurrent of modesty and loving consideration for the opinions of others. I have before spoken of His unfailing courtesy. It was really more than what that term usually connotes to the Western mind. The same Persian word is used for both reverence and courtesy. He "saw the Face of His Heavenly Father in every face" and reverenced the soul behind it. How could one be discourteous if such an attitude was held toward everyone!

The husband of 'Abdu'l-Bahá's hostess in Dublin—who, while never becoming an avowed believer, had many opportunities of meeting and talking with the Master—when asked to sum up his impressions of Him, responded, after a little consideration: "I think He is the most perfect gentleman I have ever known."

Consider. This was the verdict of a man of inherited wealth; of wide and profound culture; accustomed to judge men by delicate standards; and to whom the word *gentleman* connoted all which he held most admirable. And the term was applied by him to a man, who, it is not improbable, had never in His long life of imprisonment ever heard the word as relating to Him.

One may, perhaps, get a glimpse, if he considers deeply this rather portentous fact of what Bahá'u'lláh means when He says: "The root of all knowledge is the knowledge of God."[40] And again: "Knowledge is a single point, but the ignorant have multiplied it."[41] It may be true, as He has many times reiterated, that the only true life is that of the spirit, and that when one lives and moves and thinks constantly upon the spiritual plane, all things, both great and small, are done with perfectness.

Certainly, in my many contacts with this Master of life, I never knew Him to fail in manifesting the highest qualities of conduct, whether in the realm of material action or in intellectual or spiritual teaching.

I remember a luncheon party in Dublin, to which came a number of these summer residents to meet 'Abdu'l-Bahá. There were present a famous scientist, two well-known artists, a physician of note, and all of the fifteen or twenty people present had a background of more than one generation of wealth or culture. Could it be possible to imagine a more glaring contrast with the life 'Abdu'l-Bahá had lived?

The hostess, who had visited the Master in 'Akká while He was still a prisoner there, and whose life had become transformed through her spiritual contact with Him, has spoken to me of this gathering several times. Naturally, she was somewhat concerned that her friends whom she had known for years in the social life of Washington, Baltimore, and New York, should know the Master, to a degree at least, as she had known Him, but there was trepidation in her soul. For these men and women were not of a religious trend of thought. In fact several of them were frankly agnostic, and all were uninterested in that phase of life.

She wanted her party to be a success, of course, but more she wished these friends to get a glimpse, if only a glimpse, of that world of reality into which 'Abdu'l-Bahá had ushered her. She wondered, she has told me, how 'Abdu'l-Bahá would handle the situation, for she knew that she would not have the responsibility for its handling. 'Abdu'l-Bahá was always the host, His the dominating voice.

I was present at that gathering, but little of its true significance penetrated my consciousness. I have but the memory of a typical luncheon party where had gathered a group of society's intelligentsia to meet a noteworthy personality.

It is a perpetual wonder to me, as I recall to memory those months, during which, all unrecognized by me, the portals to spiritual freedom were slowly swinging wide, how little I understood what was really happening. I see now what a tremendous task it is to open the eyes of the blind. No wonder our Lord Christ marveled that those to whom He spake and upon whom He smiled, having eyes and ears and hearts, saw not, nor heard, nor understood. No wonder that tradition has handed down to us the confusion of thought, which must have afflicted those to whom came the revelations of the miracle of bestowed spiritual sight. To them, and even to us, too often physical sight was the great blessing; the loss of it the great tragedy; its restoration the great miracle. But to Jesus, and to all true seers, physical sight is blindness compared to the sight of the spirit. 'Abdu'l-Bahá calls it seeing by "the Light Divine" and says:

Seek with all your hearts this Heavenly Light, so that you may be enabled to understand the realities, that you may know the secret things of God, that the hidden ways may be made plain before your eyes.

This light may be likened unto a mirror, and as a mirror reflects all that is before it, so this Light shows to the eyes of our spirits all that exists in God's Kingdom and causes the realities of things to be made visible. By the help of this effulgent Light all the spiritual interpretation of the Holy Writings has been made plain, the hidden things of God's Universe have become manifest, and we have been enabled to comprehend the Divine purposes for man.[42]

Truly a miracle of miracles it is that earth-blinded eyes *ever* open to the world of reality.

Most of those present at this luncheon party knew a little of 'Abdu'l-Bahá's life history, and, presumably, were expecting a dissertation from Him on the Bahá'í Cause. The hostess had suggested to the Master that He speak to them on the subject of immortality. However, as the meal progressed, and no more than the usual commonplaces of polite society were mentioned, the hostess made an opening, as she thought, for 'Abdu'l-Bahá to speak on spiritual things.

His response to this was to ask if He might tell them a story, and he related one of the Oriental tales, of which He had a great store, and at its conclusion all laughed heartily.

The ice was broken. Others added stories of which the Master's anecdote had reminded them. Then 'Abdu'l-Bahá, His face beaming with happiness, told another story, and another. His laughter rang through the room. He said that the Orientals had many such stories illustrating different phases of life. Many of them are extremely humorous. It is good to laugh. Laughter is a spiritual relaxation. When they were in prison, He said, and under the utmost deprivation and difficulties, each of them at the close of the day would relate the most ludicrous event which had happened.

Sometimes it was a little difficult to find one but always they would laugh until the tears would roll down their cheeks. Happiness, He said, is never dependent upon material surroundings, otherwise how sad those years would have been. As it was they were always in the utmost state of joy and happiness.

That was the nearest approach He came to any reference to Himself or to the divine teachings. But over that group, before the gathering dispersed, hovered a hush and reverence that no learned dissertation would have caused in them.

After the guests had gone, and 'Abdu'l-Bahá was leaving for His hotel, He came close to His hostess and asked her, with a little wistful smile—almost, she was used to say, like a child seeking ap-probation—if she were pleased with Him.

She was never able to speak of this conclusion to the event with-out deep emotion.

'Abdu'l-Bahá was to speak in the Unitarian church that Sunday morning, but He had intimated that He would talk with me before the time for the service, so, about half-past-nine I was awaiting Him in one of the spacious private parlors of the inn.

The events of that day are among my clearest remembrances connected with the Master. At that time, about four months after my first meeting with Him, and seven months after first hear-ing of this worldwide movement, I was still, it seemed, almost as far away as ever from any true understanding of what it was all about. I was perpetually tossing in the turbulent sea of spirit: at brief moments caught in the up-thrust of that surging ocean of truth, and for an instant dazzled by the light of the Sun of Real-ity. But only for a moment; then dropped again into the trough of the sea and shut from that light. Each time the illumination came I clung to it and said within my heart: "This time I will not let Thee go." And each time, when the darkness closed around, my agonized heart averred: "The Light is gone forever. It was but a dream born of vain hopes."

I have before spoken of this inward turmoil. I speak of it again trusting that other struggling souls may find in the analysis of my experience a suggestion for a similar analysis of their own. For this servant is fully assured that every aspiring soul must fight over much the same ground. And the fight is never over, "There is no surcease in this War." For every battle won opens a wider field of combat against the never-sleeping foe of self and the contingent world.*

I often, in those days of early recognition of this fact, likened this warfare to the great war of nations even then rumbling in the Balkans. For, just as the soldier, when the zero hour strikes, plunges over his breastwork, and, through hail of shot and shell, dashes against the enemy, and, having gained what ground he can, *digs in and sticks,* never retreating, never abandoning ground once gained; so the spiritual warrior fortifies each step, each yard of ground, never looking back. Also he never forgets that far ahead lies the enemy's chief stronghold, his base of supplies, his capital city, the city of self and desire, *attachment to this world.* Not until that stronghold is completely overthrown, and the "strongly fortified fortress" of God's will and His desire attained, can any permanent and honorable peace be secured. And again he never forgets that there is a Commander in Chief directing the war, and that the "Hosts of the Supreme Concourse" are assisting him. Hence he knows that final victory is assured.

During those early and terrible days of this fighting I was at times tempted to retreat. It was not easy to face the supercilious comments of my ministerial associates, the adverse criticisms of my family and friends, the cooling goodwill of the influential members of my congregation. One of my clergymen associates asked me one

---

* In the Bahá'í terminology it means the world around us, pressing upon us, contracting us and so distracting our attention that we are apt to leave God out of our reckoning.

day: "Are you still Bahá'-ing around?" While a member of my own family told me I was a pathological case, and needed a physician.

Why I did not retreat I cannot tell. Partly, I suppose, it was because I did not realize whither the path was leading. If all that the following five or seven years were to hold, if I advanced, had been revealed to me at that time, I greatly doubt if my courage would have sufficed to brave them.

On the other hand, the glimpses I had at times of the very Glory of God; the possibilities of human attainment for the first time revealed; the happiness unspeakable that, if only for brief moments, swept over me, repaid for all the ground abandoned. I was "in the Grip of God." When in the depths, and darkness again closed around, it was so unbearable that I, perforce, must find the light again. I could not have retreated had I wished.

Some time later, to aid a friend in the throes of a similar struggle, I concocted a little fable illustrating this.

Once on a time a traveler was lost in a dense wilderness.
It seemed that for endless ages he had wandered forlorn.
No path there was; no sun by which to get his bearings.
The briers tore his flesh, the pitiless wind and rain poured down their wrath. He had no home.

Then suddenly, when hope was gone, he came out upon a mountainside overlooking a lovely valley, in which was set a heavenly palace, the very Home of his dreams.
With joy unspeakable he rushed to enter.
But hardly had his foot stepped within its precincts when a heavy hand grasped him by the neck and—back he was again in that dread wilderness.

But now he was not without hope. He had seen his home.
And with a courage unknown before, he set upon his search.

He was more careful now. He watched for signs of the Path.
And strove to pierce the overhanging gloom for gleams of light.

And, after weary search, again he saw his home.
He was more careful now. He did not rush to enter.
He noted how it lay. He oriented by the sun.
And softly his reverent feet bore him within.

But, alas, again the heavy hand tore him from that loved
home and back again he was in that vast wilderness.
But now his heart was not at all cast down.
He had his bearings! And with great joy set upon his search
again.
And now he marked the trees so he could find the path again.
The sky grew clearer overhead and gleams of sun assisted.

And soon, much sooner than before, he found his home
again, and entered.
This time he felt more calm and assured.
This time he felt no fear of grasping hand.
And when it came and grasped, and he was back in that foul
wilderness of worldly things,
he hastened with sure feet upon his search.

The Sun shone brightly now. The songs of birds entranced
his ear.
And now he beat a Path. He tore away the impeding
underbrush.
For well he knew that he would often have to tread his way
back and forth, while in this world.
But he had found his home, and when the roar of men
confused, and darkness came, he hastened back from self to
God.

That Sunday with 'Abdu'l-Bahá in Dublin was one of my days of light. He came into the room where I awaited Him and embraced me, asking if I were well and happy. We must always be happy, He said, for it is impossible to live in the spiritual world and be sad. God desires happiness for all His creatures. For man especially is this joy ordained for he has the capacity to understand reality. The world of the spirit is open to him as it is not to the kingdoms of nature below him. It is through the power of this spirit-energy that he is able to conquer nature and bend its forces to his will. God has sent His Messengers all through the ages to aid men in this conquest. I cannot recall the exact words, of course, but His point of view and the atmosphere of truth created is indelibly impressed upon my consciousness.

It was during this conversation that I asked Him again, as I often had, why I should believe in Bahá'u'lláh as the latest and most universal of these Messengers.

He looked at me long and searchingly. His smile broadened. Again He seemed to be enjoying a heavenly situation that was not without its humorous side. Then He was lovingly grave again. After a somewhat lengthy silence He said that it was not given to everyone to speak often of His Holiness Christ to men. He said that I must thank God daily for this great bounty, for men have entirely forgotten the pure teachings of this "Essence of Severance." He remarked that His Holiness Bahá'u'lláh speaks of this in the Book of Certitude and that I should study it carefully. In that book is explained how these stars of the Heaven of Christ's revelation have fallen to the earth of worldly desires. On their tongues the mention of God has often become an empty Name; in their midst His Holy Word a dead letter. This condition is that to which Christ refers, He said, when He speaks of "the oppression or affliction of the Last Days." What greater affliction could be imagined than that under which the self-appointed spiritual leaders are themselves in darkness.[43]

Praise be to God that you are seeking Light. It behooves you to manifest Light; to express in word and deed the pure teachings of His Holiness the Christ. To the proud we must be humble; He said, to the humble, compassionate; to the ignorant ones, be as a student before his master; to the sinful ones, be as the greatest sinner of all. To the poor, be a benefactor; to the orphan, a father; to the aged, a son. Take guidance, not from leaders of sectarian theology, but from the Sermon on the Mount. Seek no earthly reward, nay, rather, accept calamities in His service as His first disciples did.[44]

He smiled at me with such heavenly radiance that I sat enthralled and overcome with an emotion indescribable. Then he fell silent and His eyes closed. I thought He was weary, as doubtless He was for His constant activity gave Him little rest. But it was plain to me later that He must have been praying for me.

I, too, was still. How could I speak! I was in a world far removed from my habitual consciousness. It even, for those blissful moments, seemed possible to do as He commanded. Certainly I knew that that was what I should do, and for the first time a glimmer of the conviction came to me that I could never rest until I should approach this station to which He called me, if not in this world then in some other.

He opened His eyes after a while, smiled again, and said that all who truly seek find; that the door to the World of Reality was never closed to those who patiently knock. This is the Day of attainment.

The very atmosphere of that conventional hotel room seemed impregnated with the Holy Spirit. We sat in silence for some time and then a message came that it was time to go to the church. He embraced me again and left me.

For a little while I sat alone trying to adjust myself again to my surroundings, for I had truly been transported to another world.

Then some friends came to ask me to accompany them to the church to hear the Master's talk.

What His subject was I do not recall, nor does a single word of His address remain with me. My memory is all of the quiet New England church; the crowded pews, and 'Abdu'l-Bahá on the platform. His cream-colored robe; His white hair and beard; His radiant smile and courteous demeanor. And His gestures! Never a dogmatic downward stroke of the hand; never an upraised warning finger; never the assumption of teacher to the taught; but always the encouraging upward swing of hands, as though He would actually lift us up with them. And His voice! Like a resonant bell of finest timbre; never loud but of such penetrating quality that the walls of the room seemed to vibrate with its music.

I do remember, however, that what He said impressed me with the force of the impact of divine truth. There was not a question in my mind of the authority with which He spake. Truly, not as the scribes!

I recall that as I left the church and joined some of the New York friends who were among the audience, I said to one of them:

"At last I know. Never again will I doubt or question."

Alas, I spoke too soon. Many months too soon. My scholastic training had gone too deep. The habits of a lifetime of depending upon book learning, which, as Bahá'u'lláh says, has: "Like a gloomy dust enveloped the world,"[45] were not to be so quickly broken.

That evening I felt that I must speak to 'Abdu'l-Bahá once more. My heart was too full of thankfulness to let me rest without the effort to express it to Him. So I watched for Him to come back to the inn after His day was ended. It was quite late when at last I saw Him slowly ascending the stairs to His room.

I can hardly believe now that I had the temerity to follow. He had entered the room when I reached it, and had closed the door. What gave me courage to knock I do not know; but knock I did, and He opened the door Himself. I did not know what to say. He beckoned me in and looked at me gravely. I stammered: "Will you please pray with me?"

He motioned, and I knelt while He put His hands upon my head and chanted, in Persian, a brief prayer. It was all over within three minutes. But those moments brought to me a peace I had never known.

Before I leave the recital of the Dublin experience I will relate an incident to which I was not a witness but was told me by one who saw it. It seems that she was occupying a room in the inn at the same time that 'Abdu'l-Bahá was there. She was dressing, and happening to glance out of the window, she saw 'Abdu'l-Bahá pacing up and down dictating to His secretary. An old man, wretchedly clothed, passed the inn as she watched. 'Abdu'l-Baha sent His secretary to call him back.

The Master stepped up to him and took his hand, smiling into his face as though greeting a welcome friend. The man was very ragged and dirty. His trousers particularly were filthy and barely covered his limbs. 'Abdu'l-Bahá talked with him a few moments, His face, a smiling benediction. He seemed to be trying to cheer the old man and finally there did appear the trace of a smile, but it was rather bleak. 'Abdu'l-Bahá's eyes swept the pitiable figure, and then He laughed gently: He said something to the effect that the old man's trousers were not very serviceable and that we must remedy that lack.

It was very early in the morning and the street deserted. My friend, watching, saw 'Abdu'l-Bahá step into the shadow of the porch and He seemed to be fumbling under His 'abá at the waist. Then He stooped. His trousers dropped to the ground. He gathered his robe about Him and turning handed the trousers to the old man. "May God go with you," He said, and turned to the secretary as if nothing unusual had happened. I wonder what that man thought as he went his way. I like to think that this glimpse into a world in which someone cared enough for him to give him his own garb rather than that he should need, marked an epoch in his life, and transformed the "brass of this world into gold by the alchemy of the spirit."

During the prison-life in 'Akká, 'Abdu'l-Bahá often gave His bed to those who had none, and He always refused to own more than one coat.

"Why should I have two," He said, "when there are so many who have none?"

I mention these things in this connection to show that 'Abdu'l-Bahá did not tell others the way of life without walking therein Himself. In this incident I saw reflected indeed His advice to me in the parlor of the inn that memorable Sunday.

A few days after leaving Dublin, I wrote 'Abdu'l-Bahá, thanking Him for His courtesy and kindness. And soon there came His first Tablet* to me, in answer to my letter, which I had not thought required an answer.

It was dated August 26, 1917. I quote it in full, for the universal viewpoint from which all His words were written robs them of any personal limitation.

> O thou, my revered friend:
>
> Your letter imparted the utmost rejoicing, for its contents evidenced attraction to the Kingdom of God and enkindlement with the Fire of the Love of God!
>
> A hundred thousand ministers have come and gone: they left behind no trace nor fruit, nor were their lives productive.
>
> To be fruitless in the world of humanity is the manifest loss. A wise person will not attach his heart to ephemeral things: nay, rather, will he continually seek immortal life and strive to obtain eternal happiness.
>
> Now, praise be to God that thou hast turned thy face towards the Kingdom, and art aspiring to receive Divine Bestowals from the Realm of Might.
>
> I have become hopeful, and prayed that thou mayest attain to another Bounty; seek another Life; ask for another World;

---

* Letter.

draw nearer unto God; become informed of the Mysteries of the Kingdom; attain to Life Eternal and become encircled with the Glory Everlasting.

Upon thee be the Glory of the Most Glorious!

(signed) 'Abdu'l-Bahá 'Abbás
Written from Malden, Mass. 8/26/1912

I well remember the feelings with which I read this. It was to me then simply a beautiful letter, couched in Oriental imagery. That the last paragraph contained an actual summons to enter another world; to become truly informed of mysteries hitherto unknown; to be, in very truth and as a personal experience, encircled with the Glory Everlasting and enter, while on this little planet, into a new and higher life, so free, so vast, so joyous that only the word "eternal" would apply: all this did not dawn upon me for years.

It has become, however, increasingly apparent to me as the years have passed, that to the writer these words expressed the station in which He constantly lived, and that the great objective of His life work was to summon men to as close an approximation of that station as their capacity would permit.

CHAPTER NINE

THE AMERICAN ITINERARY. THE POWER OF THE SPIRIT. "HER HIGHNESS THE COW." TRUE GREATNESS. THE DIVINE TEACHING METHOD.

> *He is truly wise whom the world and all that is therein have not deterred from recognizing the light of this Day, who will not allow men's idle talk to cause him to swerve from the way of righteousness. He is indeed as one dead who, at the wondrous dawn of this Revelation, hath failed to be quickened by its soul-stirring breeze. He is indeed a captive who hath not recognized the Supreme Redeemer, but hath suffered his soul to be bound, distressed and helpless, in the fetters of desires.*
> —Bahá'u'lláh,
> *Gleanings from the Writings of Bahá'u'lláh,* no. 85.3

During the rest of that summer I was much occupied with work that carried me to various parts of the Eastern states while 'Abdu'l-Bahá was absent from that part of the country, making His memorable trip throughout the West.

In this interval of three months from the time of my visit to Dublin and my next meeting with the Master in New York on November 15, 'Abdu'l-Bahá had covered an itinerary and addressed audiences, which, considering His age, His historical background, and the large number of the friends who followed Him from place to place, has few parallels in history.

From the time I left His Presence in Dublin, N. H., His itinerary was as follows:

Aug. 16–24	Greenacre, Eliot, ME	5 addresses
Aug. 25–30	Boston & Maiden, MA	4
Sept. 1–10	Montreal, Canada	5
Sept. 16–19	Chicago, IL	1
Sept. 20–22	Minneapolis & St. Paul, MN	2
Sept. 24	Denver, CO	2
Oct. 1–15	San Francisco, Oakland, Palo Alto, CA	4
Oct. 18	Los Angeles, CA (no accurate record at hand). He was there 2 days at least.	3
Oct. 25 & 26	Sacramento, CA	2
Oct. 31	Chicago, IL	1
Nov. 5	Cincinnati, Ohio	1
Nov. 6–12	Washington, D. C.	10
Nov. 15–Dec. 5	New York City	13

Making a total of fifty-three addresses, besides, probably scores of personal interviews and informal talks to small groups of friends.

From the time of His arrival in this country and His Dublin sojourn, His itinerary and talks were as follows:

April 11–19	New York City	13 addresses
April 20–25	Washington, D. C.	13
Apr. 30–May 5	Chicago, IL	15
May 6	Cleveland, OH	2
May 7	Pittsburgh, PA	1
May 11–20	New York City & vicinity	7
May 23–24	Boston & vicinity	3
May 26–June 8	New York & vicinity	7
June 9	Philadelphia	2
June 11–July 15	New York & vicinity	20
July 23–25	Boston & vicinity	3
Aug. 5–6	Dublin, NH	2

(To my personal knowledge, 'Abdu'l-Bahá made several more addresses in Dublin than are recorded in the volumes of His talks published under the title *The Promulgation of Universal Peace*. But that is the official record.)

It is not simply the interest that attaches to the fact that this man, in his sixty-ninth year, was able to accomplish this rather remarkable feat of physical and intellectual endurance which prompts this catalogue of his summer's work.

There is a deeper significance to be discerned by those who attended Him during His journeyings, or even by those who have read this chronicle carefully and sympathetically. During this very summer, the poet and sage, Rabindranath Tagore, had been under contract to deliver a series of lectures in America. After covering a part of his proposed itinerary, which was not nearly as extensive as that of 'Abdu'l-Bahá's, his strength and nerves were exhausted and he cancelled his contract and returned to India. He said he could not bear the materialistic vibrations of America.* It needs also to be disclosed that while Tagore's contract called for a sizable financial remuneration, 'Abdu'l-Bahá had no contract, other than the Covenant of selfless servitude made with Bahá'u'lláh in the sanctuary of His heart, and, furthermore, so far from demanding or expecting any financial reward, He consistently refused the slightest remuneration, and even when entertained by solicitous and generous hosts He was punctilious in seeing to it that gifts to both host and servants of the household far outweighed what He received. Also He emphasized the spiritual capacity of the American people, which Tagore decried. When He stayed at hotels his "tips" to servants who waited on Him were often so generous as to excite astonishment. But even this does not at all cover what He gave. In several instances that have come to my personal knowledge His spiritual influence upon chambermaids and porters was such that

---

* He made five addresses on May 2 and three on May 5.

one of them said to one of those accompanying the Master: "This is sacred money. I shall never spend it upon myself."

Is comment necessary? Whence came the power of body, mind, and spirit that enabled this man—unused to Western bustle, competition, and nervous strain; all His long life subject to persecution, imprisonment, and hatred; cast suddenly into an environment for which he could have had no preparation—so to master every situation with which He was confronted? I have shown how this mastery extended to the details of the society of culture and luxury, but it was no less noticeable, no less victorious, when in contact with the humble and sorrowing.

How is it possible to ignore such conquering majesty! How can one refrain from searching with passionate intensity for the secret of His power! To me, after all these years of study and prayer in my search for this key, there can be only one answer, the answer given by 'Abdu'l-Bahá Himself, and even more convincingly by the Blessed Perfection, (Bahá'u'lláh). Ponder carefully the following quotations:

> Although the body was weak and not fitted to undergo the vicissitudes of crossing the Atlantic, yet love assisted us, and we came here. At certain times the spirit must assist the body. We cannot accomplish really great things through physical force alone; the spirit must fortify our bodily strength. For example, the body of man may be able to withstand the ordeal of imprisonment for ten or fifteen years under temperate conditions of climate and restful physical routine. During our imprisonment in 'Akká means of comfort were lacking, troubles and persecutions of all kinds surrounded us, yet notwithstanding such distressful conditions, we were able to endure these trials for forty years. The climate was very bad, necessities and conveniences of life were denied us, yet we endured this narrow prison forty years. What was the reason? The spirit was strengthening and resuscitating the body constantly. We lived through this long, difficult period in the utmost love and heavenly servitude. The spirit must assist the body

under certain conditions which surround us, because the body of itself cannot endure the extreme strain of such hardships.

The human body is in reality very weak; there is no physical body more delicately constituted. One mosquito will distress it; the smallest quantity of poison will destroy it; if respiration ceases for a moment, it will die. What instrument could be weaker and more delicate? A blade of grass severed from the root may live an hour, whereas a human body deprived of its forces may die in one minute. But in the proportion that the human body is weak, the spirit of man is strong. It can control natural phenomena; it is a supernatural power which transcends all contingent beings. It has immortal life, which nothing can destroy or pervert. . . . How powerful the spirit of man, while his body is so weak! . . . Therefore, it is divinely intended that the spiritual susceptibilities of man should gain precedence and overrule his physical forces. In this way he becomes fitted to dominate the human world by his nobility and stand forth fearless and free, endowed with the attributes of eternal life.[46]

The human body is in need of material force, but the spirit has need of the Holy Spirit. . . . If it is aided by the bounty of the Holy Spirit it will attain great power; it will discover realities; it will be informed of the mysteries.

The power of the Holy Spirit is here for all.

The captive of the Holy Spirit is exempt from every captivity.

The teachings of His Holiness Bahá'u'lláh are the breaths of the Holy Spirit which create man anew.

There is a Power in this Cause far, far transcending the ken of men and angels.

—Attributed to 'Abdu'l-Bahá

These few excerpts from the hundreds which might be cited will give a slight conception of the source of 'Abdu'l-Bahá's power to dominate every situation with which He was confronted.

Even His physical condition was reinforced constantly by this divine power. On one occasion after a particularly exhausting day He was returning late at night from a gathering at which He had spoken with much energy and effectiveness. In the automobile He showed great weariness. He relaxed and gradually sank into almost a comatose condition. The friends who were with Him were greatly alarmed. On arriving at their destination He had to be almost carried into the house and to His room. Within fifteen minutes, while the friends were gathered in great anxiety in the lower rooms, His voice was heard resounding with even more than its usual energy and power calling for His secretary, and He appeared at the top of the stairs His usual dominant, smiling, forceful self.

> Blessed is he that hath been enraptured by My wondrous melodies and hath rent the veils asunder through the potency of My might.[47]

To 'Abdu'l-Bahá I had written once or twice during the summer for my mind and heart gave me no rest. I carried with me on my travels through the Eastern states a small satchel devoted entirely to the books and typewritten Tablets of Bahá'u'lláh and 'Abdu'l-Bahá (of which, by the way, there is a very large available quantity besides many volumes not yet translated into English) and I, literally, read nothing else, not even newspapers, during all those months. From this fact may be gathered a faint indication of my mental and spiritual perturbation.

It seemed as though the focal center of my life had suddenly shifted, and all my interests were revolving around a new and most disturbing axis.

When my church activities were resumed in the fall I found it impossible to secure the financial support necessary to continue the work of the Brotherhood Church, and it was my letter to 'Abdu'l-Bahá telling Him of this and also of my intense and growing interest in the teachings of Bahá'u'lláh, which brought to me His second Tablet. It was evidently written on His way from Washington to New York and translated and forwarded to me from New York by His secretary immediately upon His arrival. It was as follows:

O thou spiritual friend! Thy letter was received. I was made very sad on account of the event of the closing of the Church of Brotherhood. But when I was in those parts I remarked to you that you should not place your confidence in those souls. They say many things but do not fulfill them.

You stated that "my first assistant is a philosopher." It is true that philosophy in this age consists in the fact that man is out of touch with God; he is out of touch with the Kingdom of God; he is out of touch with spiritual susceptibilities; he is out of touch with the Holy Spirit, and out of touch with the ideal verities. To wit: he may be an agnostic and a captive of the tangibilities.

In reality her highness the Cow enjoys this attribute and quality. The Cow is naturally a denier of God, a denier of the Kingdom, a denier of spiritualities and a denier of the heavenly verities. She has attained to these virtues without labor. Therefore she is the philosopher emeritus.

Our philosophers of this age after twenty years of study and reflection in the universities attain to the station of the Cow. They know only the senses as the verities.

Therefore her highness the Cow is the great philosopher, for she has been a philosopher from the beginning of her life and not after the hard mental labor of twenty years.

I have mentioned the fact to you that these promises are unstable. You should not put your trust in a soul who is without God.

In brief: be thou not unhappy. This event has happened so that thou mayest become freed from all other occupations, day and night thou mayest call the people to the Kingdom; spread the teachings of Bahá'u'lláh; inaugurate the Era of the New Life; promulgate the Reality, and be sanctified and purified from all save God. It is my hope that thou mayest become as such.

Crown thy head with this diadem of the Kingdom whose brilliant jewels have such illumining power that they shall shine upon centuries and cycles.

Ere long I shall reach New York and meet again my beloved friend. Upon thee be Bahá El Abhá! (The Glory of the Most Glorious.)

(signed) 'Abdu'l-Bahá Abbás
Translated: New York, November 14, 1912

The receipt of this Tablet left upon my mind two distinct and oddly contrasting impressions. The obvious one, of course, was its wit. It was my first personal encounter with 'Abdu'l-Bahá's wisely humorous attitude toward the accidents of life. I have already spoken of his ready laughter, especially when speaking of deeply serious things. The ordinary difficulties of daily experience, which affect most of us with sentiments of gravity, sadness, or repugnance, seemed to inspire Him to amusement.

I remember that when I met Him for the first time after the long summer's separation almost His first words were to ask if her highness the Cow were not a noble philosopher. And the smile and hearty laughter accompanying the words seemed to sum up the fundamental absurdity involved in most of "the gloomy dust arising from men of limitation enveloping the world."[48]

The second impression was gathered from the closing words of the Tablet with its command of severance, mastering and promulgating the teachings of Bahá'u'lláh all over the continent, and its assurance of divine and universal results through centuries and cycles.

It was these words, with their emphasis upon a station of such loftiness that nothing less than centuries and cycles could circumscribe its power of illumination, which gave to me the first glimmer of realization of the sort of greatness to which 'Abdu'l-Bahá referred when He said to me, as I have related, that This is a Day for *Very Great Things.*

We have quite naturally assumed that those men are great who have attained positions of prominence and power in the affairs of the world, either in the field of affairs or in the realm of the intellect. When asked to name the great ones of history: if we admire power we at once think of Julius Caesar, Napoleon, Cyrus the Great, Alexander. If we admire intellect we think of Plato, Aristotle, Herbert Spencer, Einstein.

That is to say, we judge men by our own standards: and it necessarily follows that only those who are greatest among men are able to judge *truly* what constitutes real greatness, for their standards are the highest, and they alone live up to those standards and exemplify their greatness.

How few there were during the first two centuries of the Christian era who recognized the dazzling brilliancy of the Sun of Reality in Jesus the Christ! Who would ever have associated the word "Great" with the humble fisher-folk who followed Him! Yet where are kings and empires now whose power then topped all the world! And where those humble ones!

So when that truly Great One spoke to me of this Day in which Very Great Things were to be accomplished, His vision embraced the future centuries in which the humblest of the servants of the Glory of God (Bahá'u'lláh) should shine resplendent in the Heavens of the Universe of His Revelation. What though the path to this greatness led through the scorn of men of low standards, of worldly comparisons; through every criticism and ignominy, even to martyrdom in that path, would it not be privilege enough to be associated with those who in former dispensations trod its way and found that Source of joy which is "the source of delight for all mankind"?

Truly he who would be great must be the servant of all; "the thralls of mankind." "Rejoice and be exceedingly glad for so persecuted they the Prophets before you."

I remember it was during the following winter, after 'Abdu'l-Bahá's return to the Holy Land, that one day as I was standing on the comer of Broadway and one of the downtown streets of New York, a sudden realization of this true greatness and of the fundamental futility and falsity of all earthly standards, swept over me and I said aloud, in the words of Emerson, but with a very different meaning to the words, forgetful of the crowded street: "Good-bye, proud world, *I'm going Home."*

It was the ability of 'Abdu'l-Bahá to disclose their own capacity to those souls who, sincerely seeking the way of life, asked of Him direction to the path of its attainment, which made him the supreme Teacher and set their feet upon the straight and narrow road. He never descended to the plane of the questioner except when He recognized his lack of capacity at that time for higher understanding. To such He spoke in terms conducive to his happiness on the plane occupied at the time. To a mother who anxiously inquired of Him how she should treat a difficult child, He said that she should make him happy and make him free. And this sums up the attitude he invariably assumed in dealing with a seeking soul.

Men are wandering the wilderness of time and place; caught in the net of circumstance; befooled by the illusions of sense. They are not aware of this, and that ignorance constitutes the tragedy of life. Nevertheless they long above all else to escape that wilderness in which they wander so forlorn. Under the pressure of this instinctive yearning they experiment with every path that offers the slightest hope of freedom. To the vast majority, that escape seems easiest along the path of what they call pleasure. To others, fame and power beckon, saying: "follow me and I will give you in the adulation of the world that respite from self for which you long."

To still others the refuge lies in the realms of intellect. In extending the barriers of nature; in probing into the microscopic universe; in breaking down the atom and bombarding the electron; in sweeping interstellar space with powerful and ever more powerful telescopes—all are seeking, though they know it not, for Him Who is in their very heart of hearts, "closer than their own identity." Inherently, fundamentally, essentially, inescapably dissatisfied with all the contingent world can offer they yet seek to find within its scope that answer to their questing soul and mind without which they can never find rest. They know instinctively that they must escape the self and so they seek, in flying from it to the world around them, the refuge from its grasp for which they yearn. Their longing is for an eternal home, for knowledge and love of God, but they know this not.

But 'Abdu'l-Bahá knew it, as all the Leaders of the race have known it. They know what lies deep in the heart of man. So He knew what lay hidden in the innermost heart of the questioner. Hence He answered the unspoken, not the spoken word.

When this marvelous technique of teaching began to dawn upon me I recognized for the first time the truly sublime function of any soul aspiring to lead another soul in the way of truth. I began to see why the Master of this technique seemed to evade many of my questions, speaking instead of the great opportunities of service and love in the very spot that I then occupied.

How our schools and universities would be filled with the exultant joy of eager students advancing in this path if their boards of trustees, presidents, and teachers had even the slightest glimmer of this technique of teaching! The full recognition of just one fundamental fact is all that is necessary: that every soul in the world is "distracted in search of the Friend."[49]

They do not want answers to their individual, personal, and particular questions, though they think they do. They desire one thing only: that basic truth, which will make them independent of all the manmade book-learning, which, like a "gloomy dust" rises from "men of limitation" and has enveloped them and all the world.[50]

They want the sunlight of the world of reality. They can see the path for themselves once free from the darkness of the contingent world and the "prison of self." In that glorious effulgence every question is its own answer; Heaven is found in the reaching hand; God becomes the very ear with which man hears the answer to all his queries. For when we speak of "God," we speak of truth, wisdom, the way of joyful and successful life, the "Abode of Peace," eternal life, the world of reality, for all these are synonyms of God, and to attain this knowledge should be the object of all education.

It was 'Abdu'l-Bahá's positive knowledge of this truth that enabled Him to reach the hidden divine self lying deep beneath the piled-up rubbish of the contingent world harvested by the outer mind and the fruitless energy of the functioning body. "It is my hope," He once said to me and often to others, "that thou mayest arise to such a station that no longer shalt thou need to question."

Our first personal contact with the Master after His return to New York was at a meeting of the friends in the studio of Miss Juliet Thompson in W. 10th St., where she painted the immortal portrait of 'Abdu'l-Bahá. I had become a constant attendant at the meetings of a study class held there every Friday evening, and it is largely due to these contacts that my interest was kept unflagging.

'Abdu'l-Bahá's theme that evening was twofold. First, the manifest power and majesty of Bahá'u'lláh, in that in spite of His rigorous incarceration He dominated prison walls and governors and jailers. And secondly, His conclusive demonstration that the teachings of Bahá'u'lláh contained many things never revealed by the preceding Prophets of God.

In the prison-city of 'Akká, near Mt. Carmel, Bahá'u'lláh was incarcerated for twenty-eight years, after His twelve years of exile, and His Son, 'Abdu'l-Bahá for exactly forty years. Yet from that prison Bahá'u'lláh wrote to the Sháh of Persia and to that unspeakable tyrant, 'Abdu'l-Hamid, "severely arraigning them for their oppression of their subjects and their misuse of power."[51]

> Consider how marvelous it was for a prisoner under the eye and control of the Turks to arraign so boldly and severely the very king who was responsible for His imprisonment. What power this is! What greatness! Nowhere in history can the record of such a happening be found. . . . Although a prisoner in a fortress, He paid no heed to these kings, regarded not their power of life and death, but, on the contrary, addressed them in plain and fearless language, announcing explicitly that the time would come when their sovereignty would be brought low and His own dominion be established.[52]

It is impossible to describe the majesty of 'Abdu'l-Bahá as He uttered these words. His face was illumined with a radiance not of this world. His being seemed possessed with that very power of which He spoke. It was His custom, often, to pace up and down while the measured cadences of His voice filled the room, and sentence by sentence, His words were translated by the interpreter. In this instance, however, the room being not overlarge, and crowded to its utmost capacity by the friends, there was little space for movement where He stood. Nevertheless His spiritual vitality seemed to overflow the room and it was as if (so it seemed to me, at least) He were striding its every part, searching deeply each heart. It was as if He were saying: This is that Power of which Christ spoke. The legions of angels for which He refused to call were summoned by Bahá'u'lláh, for the time foretold by Christ had come, and the King of kings had mounted His Throne.

The second subject to which He addressed Himself related to those teachings . . . Bahá'u'lláh enunciated that were absolutely new, and could be found in no revelation of past dispensations. I will not attempt to recapitulate the essence of His words. Sufficient to say that He itemized nine points in the revelation of Bahá'u'lláh which were new. "This," He said, "is in answer to those who ask: 'what is there in the teachings of Bahá'u'lláh which has not been heard before'?"

His closing words expressed the power that arises through persecution: "Pray that my enemies become multiplied," He quoted from Bahá'u'lláh's words. "They are My heralds. Pray that their number be increased and that they may cry out more loudly. The more they abuse me and the greater their agitation, the more potent and mighty will be the efficacy of the Cause of God. And eventually the gloomy darkness of the outer world will pass away and the light of Reality will shine until the whole earth will be effulgent with its glory."[53]

CHAPTER TEN

Address in the Great Northern Hotel.
The Universe of Bahá'u'lláh.
The Evolution of Man.
The Glory of Self-Sacrifice.

*I have offered up My soul and My body as a sacrifice
for God, the Lord of all worlds. I speak naught except
at His bidding, and follow naught, through the power
of God and His might, except His truth. He, verily,
shall recompense the truthful.*

—Bahá'u'lláh,
Gleanings from the Writings of Bahá'u'lláh, no. 66.2

The great assemblage gathered at the banquet in the Great Northern Hotel on the evening of November 29, marked the culmina-
tion of 'Abdu'l-Bahá's public addresses in this country. Memory
brings to mind no other occasion charged with such significances.
Here were gathered together upwards of about 600 souls. The
magnificent banquet hall was filled to its utmost capacity. All degrees of wealth and poverty; of culture and its lack; representatives
of the white, yellow, black and brown races, as well as of many
nations of the East and West, were represented.

The object of this meeting was as universal as the audience. It was not to advance any personal or political ambition; not in the interest of any social or financial group, nor any religious organization. This fact alone suffices to mark it as unique, but when we consider 'Abdu'l-Bahá's own definition of its objectives it is recognized that its exceptional nature is more than excelled by their grandeur.

This meeting of yours tonight is a universal gathering, it is heavenly and divine in purpose because it serves the oneness of the world of humanity and promotes International Peace. It is devoted to the solidarity and brotherhood of the human race, the spiritual welfare of mankind, unity of religious teaching with the principles of science and reason. It promotes love and fraternity among all mankind, seeks to abolish and destroy barriers which separate the human family, proclaims the equality of man and woman, instills divine precepts and morals, illumines and quickens minds with heavenly perception, attracts the infinite bestowals of God, removes racial, national and religious prejudices and establishes the foundation of the heavenly Kingdom in the hearts of all nations and peoples.[54]

It is difficult to assign to any one summation of the Bahá'í Faith the reason for its acceptance. Yet it is not too much to say that for me, at the stage of understanding to which I had at that time attained, it seemed that no rational mind could refuse at least its eager, instant, and alert investigation. Surely no one could deny the worthfulness of these objectives.

But the picture presented by this summary is not complete without including in it the personality and life history of Him Who spoke.

For here stood the living representative, the very incarnation of the ideals He presented so calmly. There was not one of these lofty expressions which He failed to exemplify in every word, thought, deed of His daily life. I state this, not because of that which I have read concerning His life of service from His eighth year; not because even His enemies and persecutors have united in unwilling admission of His love for them and all souls irrespective of their attitude toward Him and the Faith He loved, but I state it from my own intense scrutiny during many personal contacts with that sublime Personality.

Those who have read this chronicle with care, seeking to pierce the poor words that the underlying spirit may be revealed, will understand my meaning. The condition of spiritual insight can penetrate this meaning, "not controversy nor conflict."[55] No more could one imagine 'Abdu'l-Bahá descending to the plane of personal prejudice, animosity toward any living creature, avoidance of any rational argument, or moving and speaking under any other guidance than the indwelling all-enclosing Holy Spirit, than one could imagine the sun ceasing its shining. That which He was, He taught. That which He taught, He lived. Is it any wonder that that assemblage may be truly regarded as so unique in character as to have few, if any, parallels in history?

There is another feature of this address that impressed me deeply at the time. There was no mention whatever of the Bahá'í Faith as such, nor of Himself, nor of Bahá'u'lláh. It is as if He would say: Here are the ideals and purposes for which I stand. If you find them worthful perhaps you will wish to investigate whence comes the power which has brought them within the last sixty years before the attention of mankind, which, during all the period of recorded history, has been negligent, opposed, and scornful of every one of them. It will be time enough for you to investigate the doctrine, the philosophy, the spiritual dynamic back of the teachings, after you have approved and sought to live the life I present to you. "He that doeth the works shall know of the doctrine."

Often have I been asked the question: "Why are you a believer in the teachings of Bahá'u'lláh?" Perhaps the above summary of the outward teachings, and the descriptions of my contacts with the Teacher, will assist the reader to answer that question. But also, perhaps, a more explicit answer is required. That answer is to be found in the universal demand of the normal human being for a basic truth upon which he may found his life.

I am not a believer because of any preconceived explanation of this fundamental truth based upon the ideas of those around me, as, for instance, the Christian is such because he was brought up under its teachings, or the Muhammadan is such because he was born where those principles are prevalent, and so with all other followers of the various theologies of the world. I am first of all, humanly speaking, a rational being. I have a mind that requires intellectual satisfactions. I have found in the teachings of Bahá'u'lláh and 'Abdu'l-Bahá much more satisfactory explanations of the meaning, the origin, and the destiny of life than I have elsewhere found. I have no hesitation whatever in asserting that if tomorrow a better, more satisfying, more illuminating philosophy, a more spiritual dynamic should be presented to me, I would accept it without hesitation.

[A]nd this it seems to me is conclusive as to the reason for its acceptance. The teachings of Bahá'u'lláh comprise a veritable Universe of wisdom. It is no more possible to define its limits than for even an Einstein to define the limits of the material universe.

I remember many years ago we entertained a friend at our home who was curious to know why we had so enthusiastically accepted the Bahá'í Faith. She was a young woman of great gifts. An artist and sculptor; a cultured mind, a wide experience, and a seeking soul characterized her. She remarked after we had been conversing for some time: "But how is one to decide between the many various beliefs of humanity? I have, for instance, a Jewish friend who is just as certain that his faith comprises all that mind or heart could need as you are of the Bahá'í Faith. And I have another friend who is an ardent Christian Scientist. She cannot understand why every human being should not believe as she does. And of course many of my friends are sincere Christians, both Catholic and Protestant, who are equally certain that the tenets of their faith hold all that is necessary to life here and hereafter. The Buddhist, the Muhammadan, the Theosophist are equally certain. Who then is to decide?"

We answered: "How thankful we should be that souls in every faith are found sincerely seeking and following truth, for truth is one. But I wonder if you have found many among your friends who believe in and follow with all their hearts the teachings and example of the founders of *all* the faiths. Does your Catholic friend, for example, fully sympathize with, and sincerely love, his Protestant brother? Does your Christian Science friend accept the teachings of her Jewish friend? Can you imagine the Buddhist believer accepting and loving the Christian Scientist, the Muhammadan, and the Jew as equal participators in the Fountain of Universal Truth?"

Without hesitation she answered: "Of course not. No one could possibly do that."

"And yet," we said to her gently, "that is exactly what the Bahá'í teachings require. No one can lay the slightest claim to that title who does not accept *all* the Prophets as Mouthpieces of the One God. Their basic teachings are identical. The laws promulgated by Them differ superficially since their function is to guide men to a higher civilization, and the needs of the time demand specific applications of those eternal principles. Consequently to accept one of these Manifestations of the infinite wisdom and power is to accept all: to reject one is to reject all. That is what Bahá'u'lláh means by belief in "the Oneness and Singleness of God."

This illustrates what I mean by a conclusive reason for the rational, logical mind's acceptance of Bahá'u'lláh's teachings. The circle He draws is so inclusive that no creature is omitted, no question unanswered, no problem unsolved, no perplexity unclarified. And this is not because these intellectual, social, economic, and religious problems are minimized, but because they are simplified, reduced to their essentials, and so ordered and classified that any high-school youth may regulate his life thereby.

To illustrate: Our materialistic theory of evolution begins with the primordial cell and ends with man. This leaves a vast field absolutely untouched. The whole realm of the emotional, ethical, moral, and spiritual man becomes a sort of "no man's land." Is it any wonder that tornados of controversy have raged over this field? Bahá'u'lláh teaches that God and His creation are coeternal since there could not be imagined a Creator antedating a creation; a king without a kingdom; a general without an army. This undercuts, you see, the endless discussions as to man's origin and the beginnings of life. Whether one accepts it or not it cannot be denied that it is basic.

'Abdu'l-Bahá was once asked: which is the most important component in man's evolution, heredity or environment? He answered that both are important, but in considering the question of evolution one must always remember that man's true Father is God. Here we have a foundation for our reasoning than which no more fundamental one may be conceived. It does not exclude any intellectual or materialistic (if there is such a thing) explanation of the origin of man, but it includes the whole field which our savants leave out. It does not negate the former but it gives to it a radiant simplicity, a clarifying emotion, without which endless strife and contention ensue. And again, there is nothing in this hypothesis contrary to our most advanced scientific thinking:

"Some call it evolution and others call it God."

Here, by the way, is another illustration of Bahá'u'lláh's simplifying fundamentals. He urges man toward freedom from the entangling, confusing, strife-producing slavery to definitive words, the "Sea of Names" He calls it. He directs attention to the reality underlying all our futile attempts to characterize it and limit it.

'Abdu'l-Bahá, speaking on the subject of economics, has said: "All economic problems may be solved by the application of the

Science of the Love of God." That is to say: if the Rule called gold-
en and treated as if it were leaden (worse: for lead has its uses but
so far as one may determine, the Golden Rule has been laid on a
shelf whose dust is seldom disturbed)—if that Rule were actually applied to the world's economic problems, which if not solved
bid fair to destroy us, and the love of God, the sort of love which
makes a home life happy, were used as a *scientific* measurement to
regulate our international and national affairs; to settle all relations
between labor and capital, between rich and poor; to regulate all
coinage and commerce; can there be any doubt that the results
would be far more conducive to human welfare than our present
policies have produced?

Again: Bahá'u'lláh asserted the principle that the human race
is essentially of one stock and that the conception of the oneness
of humanity is essential to modern civilization. 'Abdu'l-Bahá in
the course of His many talks on this subject has shown conclu-
sively that all the races spring from one root-race, and that the
superficial differences of color, physiognomy, etc., are due to the
age-long influences of climate and food following on successive
migrations of the root-race. Here again, not only are we in absolute
accord with the most modern discoveries of anthropologists and
ethnologists, but, taken as a corollary to the above principles, we
have a scientific basis for approach to the problem presented by
the so-called "under-privileged," "backward," "subject" individuals
and peoples, which, once thoroughly understood and practically
applied *as a scientific discovery,* would immediately inaugurate an
international policy which in one generation could result only in
the automatic disintegration of racial, national, color, economic,
and religious prejudice with their attendant horrors of lynchings,
pogroms, expatriations, armed frontiers, together with their only
slightly lesser evils such as tariffs, money monopolies, cornering of
markets, "colonial expansion," and a legion of similar devils.

We could illustrate indefinitely but this is sufficient to explain
my point, which is that the teachings of Bahá'u'lláh are simple,

definite, easily understood by the normal mind, undeniable by the most scientific mind, workable and practical in the settlement of all modern questions, and so universal as to be applicable by any individual or peoples.

I have gone into the matter at some length because an understanding of this is essential to an answer to the question so often asked: "What is there in these teachings which I, or any other thoughtful man, may consider worthful enough to adopt?" The revelation of Bahá'u'lláh envisages an entirely new World Order based on essential and eternal principles, which, when applied, will result in a peace, prosperity, and happiness never before secured. They have a spiritual or religious foundation, of course, but these terms are used with a connotation absolutely new and in accord with all scientific investigations and human experience.

The closing words of this brief address at the banquet in the Great Northern Hotel emphasizes this fundamental criterion of values:

This meeting is verily the noblest and most worthy of all meetings in the world because of these underlying spiritual and universal purposes. Such a banquet and assemblage command the sincere devotion of all present and invite the downpouring of the blessings of God. . . . Be ye confident and steadfast; your services are confirmed by the powers of heaven, for your intentions are lofty, your purposes pure and worthy. God is the helper of those souls whose efforts and endeavors are devoted to the good and betterment of all mankind."[56]

Six days later I attended a meeting at which 'Abdu'l-Bahá spoke on the mystery of sacrifice. Ever since my first acquaintance with the Bahá'í teachings, this aspect of them had unaccountably moved my interest, as is evidenced by my questioning of the Master in the early stages of this interest concerning renunciation. (See chapter 3.)

Why this should be so I cannot determine even now, for to most of those who surrounded the Master at the time the emphasis seemed to be on the joy and happiness attending the New Birth. But to me the throes of parturition were too apparent, too agonizing, too demanding to evade notice. The cutting of the umbilical cord, which bound me to the matrix of this world, exacted such concentrated attention that little time was left, little opportunity afforded, for any true estimate of the world into which I was being ushered.

Perhaps my intense interest in the subject of self-sacrifice was founded in the clear realization, long experienced, that selfishness, egotism, pride in one's accomplishments (however limited), personal standards of values, were the great deterrents of both spiritual and material progress and peace. There was no question that those around me as well as myself—to say nothing of the underlying spirit motivating the statesmen, business leaders, courts of law and social usage—were all obsessed by this animal-self-psychology. The theologians seemed no less under its sway. Their emphasis truly was upon sacrifice but it was someone else's sacrifice, and that seemed altogether too easy a way out, to say nothing of its inherent dishonesty and utter irrationality.

And yet, that sacrifice is a principle underlying all life is plain to any thoughtful observer. The relation between food and the eater is usually considered from the standpoint of the eater alone. But surely if the food could be consulted its attitude would be quite other. It has two possibilities for a standard of judgment. It could be either that of resentment at the loss of its station of animal or vegetable, or it could be one of exultation over its change from the station of animal and vegetable matter to the station of the human organism, and the possibility offered it of becoming a working part of the muscle, nerve, and brain of man. We look upon the world of nature and see it as the battleground between the weak and the strong. But it is just as possible to view it as the field of sacrifice wherein lower or weaker forms of life become transformed into higher and stronger ones through self-sacrifice. In fact it is quite possible that one of the causes of the slow evolution of species is this very principle of sacrifice.

So when 'Abdu'l-Bahá opened His address with these words: "This evening I wish to speak to you concerning the mystery of sacrifice,"[57] my deepest attention became riveted. After pointing out that the accepted explanation of the Sacrifice of Christ is pure superstition for it appeals neither to common sense nor reason, He went on to explain the true meaning of the word, dividing it into four headings.

First: that Christ's sacrifice consisted in the willing abdication of all this world has to offer, including life itself, in order that He might lead men into the path of true life.

Had He desired to save His own life, and were He without wish to offer Himself in sacrifice, He would not have been able to guide a single soul. There was no doubt that His blessed blood would be shed and His body broken. Nevertheless, that Holy Soul accepted calamity and death in His love for mankind. This is one of the meanings of sacrifice.

As to the second meaning: He said, "I am the living bread which came down from heaven." It was not the body of Christ which came from heaven. His body came from the womb of Mary, but the Christly perfections descended from heaven; the reality of Christ came down from heaven.[58]

Consequently He meant that if any man partake of these perfections and sacrificed the perfections of the material world for the divine perfections, he would enter into the heavenly world in which Christ Himself lived, and would necessarily escape the limitations of the mortal world.

As to the third meaning of sacrifice, it is this: If you plant a seed in the ground, a tree will become manifest from that seed. The seed sacrifices itself to the tree that will come from it. The seed is outwardly lost, destroyed; but the same seed which is sacrificed will be absorbed and embodied in the tree, its blossoms, fruit and branches. If the identity of that seed had not been sacrificed to the tree which became manifest from it, no branches, blossoms or fruits would have been forthcoming. Christ outwardly disappeared. His personal identity became hidden from the eyes, even as the identity of the seed disappeared; but the bounties, divine qualities and perfections of Christ became manifest in the Christian community which Christ founded through sacrificing Himself. When you look at the tree, you will realize that the perfections, blessings, properties and beauty of the seed have become manifest in the branches, twigs, blossoms and fruit; consequently, the seed has sacrificed itself to the tree. Had it not done so, the tree would not have come into existence. Christ, like unto the seed, sacrificed Himself for the tree of Christianity. Therefore, His perfections, bounties, favors, lights and graces became manifest in the Christian community, for the coming of which He sacrificed Himself.

As to the fourth significance of sacrifice: It is the principle that a reality sacrifices its own characteristics. Man must sever himself from the influences of the world of matter, from the world of nature and its laws; for the material world is the world of corruption and death. It is the world of evil and darkness, of animalism and ferocity, bloodthirstiness, ambition and avarice, of self-worship, egotism and passion; it is the world of nature. Man must strip himself of all these imperfections, must sacrifice these tendencies which are peculiar to the outer and material world of existence.

On the other hand, man must acquire heavenly qualities and attain divine attributes. He must become the image and likeness of God. He must seek the bounty of the eternal, become the manifestor of the love of God, the light of guidance, the tree of life and the depository of the bounties of God. That is to say, man must sacrifice the qualities and attributes of the world of nature for the qualities and attributes of the world of God.[59]

May I ask the reader to note the ascending scale of these definitions, and the final emphasis upon the individual's responsibility if he is to achieve this final station of perfection? Here is no dependence on another's sacrifice. The call is to you and me to abandon, at whatever cost, the world of the animal, the beastly, the material man, in order that we may enter this world of reality, unsubject to the laws of time, place, and decay. And how logical! How simple it is all made. Could anything be more beautiful, more winning, than His illustration of the sacrifice of the iron to the fire:

For instance, consider the substance we call iron. Observe its qualities; it is solid, black, cold. These are the characteristics of iron. When the same iron absorbs heat from the fire, it sacrifices its attribute of solidity for the attribute of fluidity. It sacrifices its attribute of darkness for the attribute of light, which is a quality of the fire. It sacrifices its attribute of coldness to the quality of heat which the fire possesses so that in the iron there remains no solidity, darkness or cold. It becomes illumined and transformed, having sacrificed its qualities to the qualities and attributes of the fire.

Likewise, man, when separated and severed from the attributes of the world of nature, sacrifices the qualities and exigencies of that mortal realm and manifests the perfections of the Kingdom, just as the qualities of the iron disappeared and the qualities of the fire appeared in their place.

Every man trained through the teachings of God and illumined by the light of His guidance, who becomes a believer in God and His signs and is enkindled with the fire of the love of God, sacrifices the imperfections of nature for the sake of divine perfections. Consequently, every perfect person, every illumined, heavenly individual stands in the station of sacrifice. It is my hope that through the assistance and providence of God and through the bounties of the Kingdom of Abhá you may be entirely severed from the imperfections of the world of nature, purified from selfish, human desires, receiving life from the Kingdom of Abhá and attaining heavenly graces. May the divine light become manifest upon your faces, the fragrances of holiness refresh your nostrils and the breath of the Holy Spirit quicken you with eternal life.[60]

As these closing words fell upon my ears it seemed for the first time in the long years of search and struggle that a sure and attainable goal was in sight. Is it possible to imagine any price one would not pay for this attainment? For the goal is nothing less than perfection.

And here something must be interpolated as to the meaning of "perfection" in the Bahá'í terminology. It must never be overlooked that the substratum underlying all 'Abdu'l-Bahá's statements is logical and scientific. Nothing is ever stated (at least this is true in principle) that is not susceptible of proof. In using this word "perfection," for instance, the principle of relativity is recognized. Jesus' statement that: "There is none good save God," is understood as a scientific axiom: That is, perfection is seen as impossible except to the Unconditioned, the "Self-subsistent," all other perfection is relative. We speak of a perfect rose. We do not mean that a more beautiful, more satisfying one cannot be imagined, but simply that so far as our experience goes that rose, at that particular moment, strikes us as the most beautiful one, the most perfect one, we have ever seen. Nor do we, when we speak of the rose as occupying that position, contrast this perfection, or include it, with or in any category comprehending other objects than the rose, or even any other than that particular color or type of rose. We may in the next moment speak of a perfect sunset, or a perfect baby, or a perfect action, but always with the same reservation of relativity.

So when we speak of a perfect man. We do not mean, nor could we possibly ever mean, no matter to what heights of nobility he may have attained, that he could not be more noble, more "perfect." We simply mean that the heights to which he has attained, compared to the average standards of human behavior, are more nearly our ideal than we have heretofore met.

So then it resolves itself into a question of personal and individual standards, or units of measurement. The gangster's ideal of perfection would be quite other than Abraham Lincoln's. Each soul must create, or absorb, an ideal of perfection that is at once within reach and satisfying to himself.

The difference between the Bahá'í ideal and any heretofore presented lies in the fact that the Bahá'í program includes *group* perfection. It involves the postulate of man as a gregarious, a social, a cosmopolitan, an international, a *world* being. A perfect man, then, under this category, must simply have attributes that will, if extended to a sufficient number of individuals, result in a World Order, the goal of which is the elimination of those factors which have in the past, and still have, resultants tending toward relative imperfections both in the individual and society.

In the use of the word "perfection," (see bottom of page 131) I mean that for the first time the ideals held for many years as a Christian believer, of approximating my rules of conduct to those laid down and exemplified by the Christ, came within the purview of possibility, of probability—nay, of certainty. I said to myself: "If it should take a hundred thousand years, in this life or in some other, it can be done and must be done."

At that time the "World Order" of Bahá'u'lláh had not been elaborated, although it had been visioned implicitly in the writings of Bahá'u'lláh, and since been elaborated and explained by 'Abdu'l-Bahá. But it was even then plain to any clear thinking person that such perfections of individual attainment needed only sufficient extension of acceptance and approximation to make the present world *disorder* of war, crime, poverty and confusion if not impossible at least much decreased. In fact, the words of Bahá'u'lláh and of 'Abdu'l-Bahá are filled with glowing descriptions of world conditions when these ideals are put into practice.

This world shall become as a garden and a paradise.

This mound of earth shall become the mound of heaven.

Perhaps it was the clear explication of the results accruing to one attaining the "station of sacrifice" that stirred me most deeply. Freedom from the lower, the animal, the selfish, the egoistic self! What a Goal to hold before the mind. And no longer was it a vague, illusory goal. It had become, for that moment of clear insight at least, a goal in sight, an attainable goal.

Moreover the very word "sacrifice" had become alluring. No longer did it connote suffering, deprivation. It was clearly seen as the exchange of something less worthful for something infinitely more worthful. It had become, not a giving up of desirables, but the acquisition of desirables. Instead of a doubtful proposition in which the profit was intangible and uncertain, it had assumed the proportions of a clear-cut business proposition. I was in the market for pearls. I had now my eye on the Pearl of Greatest Price.

CHAPTER ELEVEN

INSTRUCTION IN THE WAY OF LIFE.
WHAT IS AUTHORITY?
THE SCIENCE OF THE LOVE OF GOD.

*The Ancient Beauty hath consented to be bound with
chains that mankind may be released from its bondage, and hath accepted to be made a prisoner within
this most mighty Stronghold that the whole world may
attain unto true liberty. He hath drained to its dregs
the cup of sorrow, that all the peoples of the earth may
attain unto abiding joy, and be filled with gladness.*
—Bahá'u'lláh,
Gleanings from the Writings of Bahá'u'lláh, no. 45.1

As the day drew near which should mark the close of 'Abdu'l-Bahá's
visit in America, the thought of His departure and the consequent
end of the possibility of speaking to Him, of even a few words
with Him, even of the privilege, inestimable it had grown to seem
to me, of watching Him as He spoke or moved, or sat silent while
others spoke, became increasingly insupportable. I fear that the
first five days of December, 1912, my home and church people
saw little of me. Wherever He was, there was I, if by any juggling
of hours and duties it could possibly be managed. The only occasion I missed was His address before the Theosophical Society the

evening before He sailed, which fell on a night when I was unavoidably busy elsewhere. But for the rest, day and night, I haunted the home at 780 West End Ave., where 'Abdu'l-Bahá spent those last days with the friends to whom I have often referred in this narrative, who had placed all that they had at His disposal during His stay in the country.

One of the occasions that stands out most vividly in my memory was on the afternoon of December 2 when the Master, in the presence of a group of the friends, spoke to us words so enthralling, so simple, so impressive and stimulating to the highest in man's nature, that I can find no parallel save in the last words of Jesus to His disciples. I confidently leave it to the reader whether this comparison is justified. He spoke very briefly: about 300 words as they are recorded in the collection of His addresses in this country. I shall quote them in full. They are worth it. But no record of the words themselves, moving and uplifting as they are, could possibly convey the majesty, the gentleness, the humility, the love, that animated them. I sat very close to Him and it seemed there flowed from Him to me a veritable stream of spiritual energy, which at times was overpowering. After a few words to the effect that since these were His last days with us He wished to give us His "last instructions and exhortations" and that these "were none other than the teachings of Bahá'u'lláh," He continued:

> You must manifest complete love and affection toward all mankind. Do not exalt yourselves above others, but consider all as your equals, recognizing them as the servants of one God. Know that God is compassionate toward all; therefore, love all from the depths of your hearts, prefer all religionists before yourselves, be filled with love for every race, and be kind toward the people of all nationalities. Never speak disparagingly of others, but praise without distinction. Pollute not your tongues by speaking evil of another. Recognize your enemies as friends,

and consider those who wish you evil as the wishers of good. You must not see evil as evil and then compromise with your opinion, for to treat in a smooth, kindly way one whom you consider evil or an enemy is hypocrisy, and this is not worthy or allowable. You must consider your enemies as your friends, look upon your evil-wishers as your well-wishers and treat them accordingly. Act in such a way that your heart may be free from hatred. Let not your heart be offended with anyone. If someone commits an error and wrong toward you, you must instantly forgive him. Do not complain of others. Refrain from reprimanding them, and if you wish to give admonition or advice, let it be offered in such a way that it will not burden the bearer. Turn all your thoughts toward bringing joy to hearts. Beware! Beware! lest ye offend any heart. Assist the world of humanity as much as possible. Be the source of consolation to every sad one, assist every weak one, be helpful to every indigent one, care for every sick one, be the cause of glorification to every lowly one, and shelter those who are overshadowed by fear.

In brief, let each one of you be as a lamp shining forth with the light of the virtues of the world of humanity. Be trustworthy, sincere, affectionate and replete with chastity. Be illumined, be spiritual, be divine, be glorious, be quickened of God, be a Bahá'í.[61]

In these days of unfaith when the world of intellect is obsessed with delusions of its own infallibility, when science has abrogated all dependence upon other than its own findings; when the very word "authority," as the source of any truth, is anathema even to the most thoughtful and spiritual amongst them, words such as these shine like the sun rising upon a very dark world.

If it may be allowable to question these ignorant ones, "the simple, whom they call savants,"[62] to quote Bahá'u'lláh's own words, I would like one or all of them to submit a definition of "authority." Do they absolve themselves from *all* dependence upon it or only from that form of authority that deals with matters relating to what the five senses may apprehend? Do they accept Aristotle and Newton and Hegel and Spencer and Einstein as "authorities" in their fields but refuse to accept Moses and Buddha and Jesus and Muhammad and Bahá'u'lláh and 'Abdu'l-Bahá as authorities in Theirs? Do they postulate before they begin to think, . . . that there are no such things in man's experience as wife and child and friend and home where love and self-sacrifice are assumed as integral parts of man's nature? Do they cancel out all aspiration, all love of beauty and truth, all heroism and remorse?

"Ah, but you go too fast," I hear one remonstrate. "We do not accept any of these men of whom you speak as 'authorities' in their chosen field. If we should, gone would be all progress, all invention, all hope for further truth. We accept such as 'authorities' only until they have been disproven as such. When Einstein and Minkowski, for instance, published their revolutionary ideas, which changed all our notions regarding space and time, and a little later Rutherford introduced ideas equally changing our fundamental conceptions of matter, we did not accept them as 'authorities.' Quite the contrary. They were pounced upon and subjected to the piercing inquiry of every scientist in the world. It was only after this, and even then subject to the reservation of future discovery, that they were hailed as *provisional* authorities. A new factor may be introduced at any moment entirely altering the foundation upon which their structure of hypothesis is reared. That is why we refuse to accept in the realm of the immaterial what we cannot accept in the realm of the senses."

If I have not quoted you accurately, yet it seems to me that this is what you must say, for it is the status to which the scientific thinker is reduced. And I would farther ask him, then, if by any chance he actually believes that the modern thinker along spiritual and nonmaterial lines takes any different attitude toward what he calls revealed truth? Certainly the Bahá'í does not.

The first principle under which the consistent Bahá'í thinker acts is *"The independent investigation of truth."* This is definitely urged, I had almost said commanded, by Bahá'u'lláh. 'Abdu'l-Bahá, in explaining this fundamental tenet says:

> Religion must conform to science and reason; otherwise, it is superstition. God has created man in order that he may perceive the verity of existence and endowed him with mind or reason to discover truth. Therefore, scientific knowledge and religious belief must be conformable to the analysis of this divine faculty in man.[63]

And again:

> If religion is opposed to reason and science, faith is impossible; and when faith and confidence in the divine religion are not manifest in the heart, there can be no spiritual attainment.[64]

And yet again:

> God has bestowed the gift of mind upon man in order that he may weigh every fact or truth presented to him and adjudge whether it be reasonable.[65]

And finally, though such citations could be multiplied almost indefinitely: *"It were better to have no religion than a religion which did not conform to reason."*

That is to say the modern religious thinker's definitions of "authority" conform in every respect to the scientist's own definitions. Nothing is accepted until passed through the alembic of man's reason. The only difference lies in the fact that the Bahá'í (a term that simply connotes a true seeker after Light, who loves the Light from whatever Lamp it shines) extends the limits of his search for truth to include not only the resources of the senses but the equally, if not superior, important spheres of the emotions, the ideals, the aspirations, and longings of the human soul and spirit.

I have long inwardly fretted against the assumption of the self-styled "intellectuals" that the field of "science" was bounded solely by the realm of sense-impression. Why should not the word *science* include the whole field of man's experience? Someone has said that nothing may be proved that is worthy of proof. If anyone should suggest to you or to me that our love for wife or child has no existence because it cannot be subjected to proof by the microscope, I think we might reasonably consider that an insulting remark had been made. Yet as a matter of fact, love is just as susceptible of "proof as is the law of gravitation, which, by the way, our modern scientists are now proceeding to cast doubt upon. But they do not dare to cast doubt on the phenomenon of love and its various manifestations in the racial experience of man, for it is susceptible of the proof offered by the total field of that experience.

So when I unhesitatingly accept such words as are quoted here as "authoritative" in matters dealing with the ideal and satisfactory life, it is only after they have passed the bar of my reason and judgment. Surely these adjurations are not unreasonable. The mind will find some difficulty in denying their simple rationality. Nor could the emotions, the "heart," reject them as puerile and unsatisfying. Nor could experience as we know it personally, or through racial history, deny their success when applied to the affairs of men; else Marcus Aurelius, Epictetus, Emerson, and a host of their ilk are foolish chasers of the wind.

If, then, the authorities in the field of material science are such only in the accepted sense that they are subject to the challenge of individual reason, and the Bahá'í (any sincere and unprejudiced seeker after truth) defines his authority in the same terms; if both hold such authorities as subject to displacement by a higher truth if it should be presented, and if the field covered by one of these "authorities" is far wider than the other, far more satisfying to the whole nature of man, far more remunerative in terms of actual living, it would seem to me that not only have we reason to designate both as operating within the realms of "science" but that that which covers the widest realm must be the greatest, the most fundamental of all "sciences."

CHAPTER TWELVE

The Center of the Covenant.
The New World Order.
A Divine Civilization.
The Kingdom of God on Earth.

*The world's equilibrium hath been upset through the
vibrating influence of this most great, this new World
Order. Mankind's ordered life hath been revolution-
ized through the agency of this unique, this wondrous
System—the like of which mortal eyes have never
witnessed.*

—Bahá'u'lláh,
Gleanings from the Writings of Bahá'u'lláh, no. 70.1

On the evening of the same day, December 2, 'Abdu'l-Bahá spoke
to a large group of the friends in the same home referred to in the
previous chapter. His theme covered the spiritual teachings peculiar to the revelation of Bahá'u'lláh. It is essential to the complete
understanding of the reader of the influences, which have exerted
such a revolutionary effect upon the life of the writer, that the
words of 'Abdu'l-Bahá on this subject should be elaborated a bit.

And here I must digress a little to explain why I have forced myself to write so frankly of the personal and intimate things, which,

had I followed my own inclinations, would have been locked deep within my heart. There is only one reason. For many years I have striven to evade the responsibility that this obligation has laid upon me, and which, under the repeated urging of friends I can no longer do. The reason is this:

Humanity is one. No individual is without a spiritual, as well as a physical relationship with every other individual. The hopes, longings, aspirations of one are those of each and all. The depths and heights; the agonies and joys; the victories and defeats vary in intensity with each individual according to the capacity and courage of each, but all travel much the same path and all fight over much the same ground.

If, then, one of these units in the struggling, aspiring mass has found the path to the "Abode of Peace"; has won battles, if not the whole campaign, in this universal field, and, knowing that so many of his worldwide brothers are still "distracted in search of the Friend"; still so unnecessarily and despairingly involved in a dying civilization to whom a new courage and hope and energy might be conveyed by a knowledge of the way out of the wilderness found by one who has fought over the very ground upon which they are more or less aimlessly and hopelessly fighting, should not the history of that campaign be recounted that other souls, bewildered and saddened as I was, might, God willing, be ever so little assisted in meeting and overcoming the same army of spiritual enemies? It seems to me that this is a responsibility that may not be evaded— hence this history.

This chapter is devoted to a summary of the teachings of Bahá'u'lláh as given by 'Abdu'l-Bahá on that memorable evening.

He began by saying that he would mention *some* of the teachings which are peculiar to Bahá'u'lláh's teachings: saying that in addition to those He is about to mention there are many others which are to be found in the books, Tablets, and epistles written by Bahá'u'lláh such as the Hidden Words, Glad Tidings, Words of Paradise, Tablet of the World and the Aqdas, or Most Holy Law, which cannot be found in any of the past books or epistles of other prophets.

"A fundamental teaching of Bahá'u'lláh," He began, "is the oneness of the World of Humanity."

> Addressing mankind He said: "Ye are all leaves of one tree and the fruits of one branch." By this it is meant that the world of humanity is like a tree, the nations and peoples are the different limbs or branches of that tree and the individual human creatures are as the fruits and blossoms thereof. In all the religious teachings of the past the human world has been represented as divided into two parts, one the "people of the Book" (followers of some particular Prophet) or the pure tree, and the other the people of infidelity and error, or the evil tree. The former were considered as belonging to the faithful and the others to the hosts of the irreligious and infidel; one part of humanity the recipients of divine mercy and the other the object of the wrath of their Creator. His Holiness Bahá'u'lláh removed this by proclaiming the oneness of the world of humanity and this principle is specialized in His teachings for He has submerged all mankind in the sea of divine generosity. Some are asleep; they need to be awakened. Some are ailing; they need to be healed. Some are immature as children; they need to be trained. But all are recipients of the bounty and bestowals of God.[66]

I submit to the reader whether or not the application of this principle to the problems of international statesmanship, commerce, and religion would or would not conduce to the happiness and prosperity of mankind.

I suggest that the reader, if he questions the scientific accuracy of the statement (i.e., the implied assertion that all races and colors have the same capacity for mental and spiritual advancement; that all are affected by the same handicaps and freed by the same method), consult some recognized up-to-date ethnologist on the matter.

"Another new principle," 'Abdu'l-Bahá went on, "is the injunction to investigate Truth—that is to say, no man should blindly follow his ancestors and forefathers. Nay, each must see with his own eyes, hear with his own ears and investigate the truth himself in order that he may follow the truth instead of blind acquiescence and imitation of ancestral beliefs."[67]

In the previous chapter I have pointed out how deeply this affects the traditional connotations of the word "authority," but consider how it also affects the connotations mankind has throughout historical times associated with the words *religion, law, government, education*. In fact, there is hardly a single angle of our social, economic, or religious life that is not dominated by what somebody in the remote past has had to say on the matter. We are ruled in law by the precedents laid down either by Roman or Anglo-Saxon jurisprudence. The very phraseology in which our legal documents are couched smacks of the dust of courtrooms of a thousand years ago or more. We are ruled in educational fields by precedents established when students and teachers alike were living under conditions, and motivated by ideals, as different from those of today as could well be imagined.

But why continue? The facts are pikestaffian. And this monstrous slavery under which we attempt to carry on in a world of radio-airplane-Soviet newness is not confined to the so-called thoughtless mob. It is true that for some centuries yet, the vast majority of mankind will be content to follow rather than lead. As James Truslow Adams remarks: "Within any appreciable period of time to expect it ('the vast herd') to reason like John Dewey is as irrational as to expect it to carve like Phidias or paint like Rembrandt. It will be guided by its desires and emotions." But when this subordination of one mind to another, which functioned possibly 2,000 years ago, extends to the intellectual, educational, governmental, religious, and legal leaders of the race it behooves us to consider carefully what kind of ground lies at the bottom of the precipice toward which we are all rushing so madly. How hard is the ground? How destructive will be the certain smashup of a civilization that insists on being guided by superstition rather than by reason?

How simply, nobly, *scientifically* Bahá'u'lláh places His finger on the crucial spot!

> "O Son of Spirit! The best beloved of all things in My sight is Justice; turn not away therefrom if thou desirest Me, and neglect it not that I may confide in thee. By its aid thou shalt see with thine own eyes and not through the eyes of others, and shalt know of thine own knowledge and not through the knowledge of thy neighbor. Ponder this in thy heart; how it behooveth thee to be. Verily justice is My gift to thee and the sign of My loving-kindness. Set it then before thine eyes."[68]

Again I ask the reader to consider what effect would in all likelihood be produced upon civilization if the leaders of world thought could suddenly become convinced that the Author of this sublime paragraph was one of the long line of divinely inspired Prophets, Who has appeared in the world at this time to act as the Leader of the race in the establishment of a New World Order, and one of Whose fundamental precepts directs each individual's attention to *his own* responsibility. Consider how the application of this one principle would affect the immediate overthrow of the abuses in the fields of religion, law, education, and government. Backed by the emotional impulse of the love of God (love of the new Messiah enshrined within the earthly Temple of the "Glory of God"), it is impossible to predict the beauty and joy of the civilization, which, within the space of two or three generations, would be established.

'Abdu'l-Bahá continued:

Bahá'u'lláh has announced that the foundation of all the religions of God is one, that oneness is truth and truth is oneness which does not admit of plurality. This teaching is new and specialized to this Manifestation.

He sets forth a new principle for this day in the announcement that religion must be the cause of unity, harmony and agreement among mankind. If it is the cause of discord and hostility, if it leads to separation and creates conflict, the absence of religion would be preferable in the world.

Furthermore, He proclaims that religion must be in harmony with science and reason. If it does not conform to science and reconcile with reason, it is superstition.[69]

It is unnecessary to enlarge upon the wisdom and common sense of these principles or to speak of the practical results accruing from their application. Surely they are apparent.

He establishes the equality of man and woman. This is peculiar to the teachings of Bahá'u'lláh, for all other religions have placed man above woman.[70]

In commenting upon this I simply point out that this principle, as enunciated by the Founder of the Bahá'í Faith, was laid down as early as 1853, and in a country, Persia, which from time immemorial had placed women on a level with the animal and denied them even the possession of a soul. It was about 1848 that there arose in Persia a woman who could well be styled the first woman suffragist, Qurratu'l-'Ayn (Consolation of the Eyes). She was the only woman among the eighteen disciples of the Báb, the divine forerunner of Bahá'u'lláh.

"She threw aside her veil," says 'Abdu'l-Bahá, "carried on controversies with the most learned men, and in every meeting she vanquished them. She was stoned in the streets, exiled from town to town, threatened with death, but she never failed in her determination to work for the freedom of her sisters. She bore persecution with the greatest heroism and even in prison gained converts. To a Persian minister, in whose house she was imprisoned, she said: You can kill me as soon as you like but you cannot stop the emancipation of women. At last she was strangled and her body thrown into an empty well and stones piled upon it. Preparing for her execution she put on her choicest robes as if she were going to a bridal party."[71]

So speaks 'Abdu'l-Bahá of this heroic leader of women who gave her life for the liberation of her sex at a time when Susan B. Anthony, Frances Willard , and others had not yet begun the campaign.

A new religious principle is that prejudice and fanaticism— whether sectarian, denominational, patriotic or political—are destructive to the foundation of human solidarity; therefore, man should release himself from such bonds in order that the oneness of the world of humanity may become manifest.[72]

The cancer at the heart of world society is prejudice. It affects every relation in life from "other-side-of-the-tracks" snobbery to racial and religious antagonisms resulting in lynchings, pogroms, and massacres like that of St. Bartholomew and the centuries-long persecution of the Armenians. I do not ask the reader to believe that such a cancer may at once be eradicated, but only to ask himself whether it might not have a fair chance of extermination if an influential minority of world leaders, who would necessarily carry with them the mass of their followers, became convinced (after scientific investigation) of the "authority" of the promulgator of this principle.

"Universal peace," 'Abdu'l-Bahá went on, "is assured by Bahá'u'- lláh as a fundamental accomplishment of the religion of God—

that peace shall prevail among nations, governments and peoples, among religions, races and all conditions of mankind. This is one of the special characteristics of the Word of God revealed in this Manifestation."[73]

This is what Bahá'u'lláh calls "The Most Great Peace." Note that it implies not the mere cessation of warfare. It goes to the root of the matter and envisages the whole composite life of the individual, the society in which he functions, and the emotions which are the mainsprings of action.

"Bahá'u'lláh declares that all mankind should attain knowledge and acquire an education."[74]

Again I would point out that this principle found utterance at a time when education in all parts of the world was assumed to be the prerogative only of a certain class. Its acquirement was denied the millions of children and adults alike whose station in life cut them off from those privileges of intellectual attainments that are the source of power. It was rightfully discerned that if the underdogs should be allowed the same access to the sources of this power, which their rulers possessed, their writhings might displace the mighty from their seats. It is an interesting coincidence, to say the least, that with this commanding edict from Bahá'u'lláh began the first emergence of what is known as free education of "the common people," and with it the first hopeful efforts toward their freedom in every field of human activity.

He has set forth the solution and provided the remedy for the economic question. No religious Books of the past Prophets speak of this important human problem.

He has ordained and established the House of Justice, which is endowed with a political as well as a religious function, the consummate union and blending of church and state. This institution is under the protecting power of Bahá'u'lláh Himself. A universal, or international, House of Justice shall also be organized. Its rulings shall be in accordance with the commands and teachings of Bahá'u'lláh, and that which the Universal House of Justice ordains shall be obeyed by all mankind. This international House of Justice shall be appointed and organized from the Houses of Justice of the whole world, and all the world shall come under its administration.[75]

That is to say: Bahá'u'lláh has planned and ordained a type of world organization that bears an analogous relation to the Federal Government of the United States in that it envisages a federation of the nations of the world under a central "House of Justice." There is this important and far-reaching difference, however—the Plan of Bahá'u'lláh involves that this governing head shall have a religious as well as a political function. This startles the minds of those who associate "religion" with the history of the abuses growing out of the warfare between Muhammadans and Christians, between Catholics and Protestants, and the only lesser strife between the countless sects in all religions.*

---

* A comprehensive analysis of the Bahá'í World Commonwealth envisioned in the writings of Bahá'u'lláh is beyond the scope of this volume; however, the subject is elaborated on a great deal in the writings of Shoghi Effendi, the Faith's Guardian. Shoghi Effendi explains the ways in which the Faith's administrative system differs from the various forms of governance prevalent in the world, stressing that while the system "can never be identified with any of the standard types of government referred to by Aristotle in his works," it "embodies and blends with the spiritual verities on which it is based the beneficent elements which are to be found in each one of them." He goes on to state that the "evils inherent in each system are rigidly and permanently excluded" from the Bahá'í system.

From a Bahá'í perspective, this vision of the distant future, which repudiates excessive centralization and upholds individual rights, may only occur as a supremely voluntary and democratic process among the peoples of the world, and is predicated on major evolutionary developments in the world over time in which both unity and the appreciation for diversity are far more highly developed at every level of human society. See Shoghi Effendi, *The World Order of Bahá'u'lláh*. Wilmette, IL: Bahá'í Publishing Trust, 1991 [pp. 152–54].

But when it is understood that *this* state religion formulated by Bahá'u'lláh is predicated upon world unity in the spheres of social, economic, and educational activities as well as of religion; when one realizes that "the rulings of the House of Justice shall be in accordance with the commands and teachings of Bahá'u'lláh," which abolish prejudice, bigotry, and contention; it is seen that the objections to such a union tend to disappear.

To draw a parallel, let us assume that at the time of the Council of Nicea in 325 A.D., a constitution had been drawn up for the government of the Holy Roman Empire based upon the Sermon on the Mount, the thirteenth chapter of 1st Corinthians; the twelfth chapter of Romans, the Epistles of John; and a few scattering paragraphs of similar high ethical import from the Old Testament. Let us suppose further that included in that constitution had been the principle that the prophets of all other religions were of equal authority with Christ and Moses; that Zoroaster and Krishna and Buddha were accepted as of equal authority with the Christ, and that all Their followers were included among the participants of the benefits accruing to this unity of peoples and religions under the Holy Roman Empire. And still further let us suppose that Christ Himself had left a written constitution to the above effect and had appointed under His own hand and seal a certain one of His disciples as the first head of the governing council of the Empire, together with a definite program for the selection of His successors, the tenure of these incumbents to be determined by a cabinet, or council elected by popular suffrage by all the peoples of the then known world. If your imagination is active enough to suppose all this, your honest judgment will follow that the history of religion for the last nineteen hundred years would have been vastly different.

Yet all that I have ventured to put as a supposition in the case of Christianity, falls short of the facts underlying the establishment of the Bahá'í World Religion. This, I think, will be demonstrated later in this chapter.

The last one of the distinguishing characteristics of the revelation of Bahá'u'lláh that 'Abdu'l-Bahá elaborated that evening is one that is not usually emphasized, yet it is of the utmost importance. 'Abdu'l-Bahá called it "*the most great characteristic*" of the teachings of Bahá'u'lláh.

> It is the ordination and appointment of the Center of the Covenant. By this appointment and provision He has safeguarded and protected the religion of God against differences and schisms, making it impossible for anyone to create a new sect or faction of belief. To insure unity and agreement He has entered into a Covenant with all the people of the world designating the interpreter and explainer of His teachings so that no one may interpret or explain the religion of God according to his own view or opinion and thus create a sect founded upon his individual understanding of the divine words.[76]

That is to say: Bahá'u'lláh in His Will and Testament named His own Son, 'Abdu'l-Bahá, as the sole interpreter of the meaning and implications of His teachings. "He did this," He said, "not because he is My son but because he is the purest channel in the world for the dissemination of the Water of Life."

To make the picture complete it is necessary to include in this explanation a reference to the Will and Testament, which 'Abdu'l-Bahá left when He passed from this world in 1921. In that Will He appointed His grandson, Shoghi Effendi, then a youth of twenty-four, as Guardian of the Cause of God and the Head of the first House of Justice. One of the prime functions of the Guardian is to decide without question as to the meanings and implications of the teachings of Bahá'u'lláh.

Now let us use our most vivid imagination again. Let us suppose that Peter, instead of being a fisher-disciple of Jesus, had been His own son, had been under His care and instruction since infancy. Let us watch Jesus as He grew to old age writing innumerable books, and epistles and holding countless conversations with His followers who had grown before His passing to a host numbering in the hundreds of thousands, and had seen thousands of believers die as martyrs in His Cause, in spite of the fact that He was in exile and prison for the last forty years of His life.

And let us finally postulate that Peter, His son, lived for twenty-nine years after the passing of Jesus (remembering that Jesus had left the appointment of this son as the only interpreter of His words) and that those years had been spent in writing books, thousands of letters answering every conceivable question that could arise as to the meaning of the teachings of Jesus, and finally that Peter had spent some ten years traveling throughout the known world, meeting not scorn and persecution but honor and respect from all classes of people. Then, as has been said, before his own passing at the age of seventy-seven years, appointing his grandson to act as the Guardian of the purity of Jesus' teachings.

I think you will agree with me that not only would the history of the Christian Church have been more free from the schisms that have rent it asunder, but that the Holy Roman Empire would have been a power for unity and peace, acting ever for the welfare and happiness of the race; for do not forget that its constitution would have been based solely on the words of the Prophets of God, culminating in the Sermon on the Mount, and that no discrimination was allowable between the followers of any one of these Mouthpieces of the Eternal.

I have followed this hypothetical analogy at some length for it seems to me the best form in which to present vividly the World Order planned and ordained by Bahá'u'lláh, explained, exemplified and fully set forth by 'Abdu'l-Bahá, and which is now being actively brought into functioning power by Shoghi Effendi.

There is still one highly important feature of the plan of Bahá'u'lláh that needs emphasis. He has ordained in His law that throughout the world there shall be built Temples for the worship of the one God, in which all mankind shall be welcomed, without regard to the name under which they have chosen to be enrolled. These Temples consist of ten buildings; a central one built after a prescribed plan, having nine sides, nine entrances, nine paths radiating from these entrances leading to the nine other buildings surrounding the central House of Worship. These nine buildings are to represent and typify the various means by which the Love of God flows forth in manifestation of the love of man for man. For instance a hospital, an institution of learning, a home for the aged, an institution for the care and instruction of the blind, a home for orphaned children, a laboratory for scientific research, an institution for the care and instruction of the deaf and dumb and subnormal unfortunates, and a building containing lecture halls and classrooms for the dissemination of the principles and objectives of pure religion, for this is not within the functions of the House of Worship itself. Within those holy walls the words of man are never heard. No sermons or ritual observances are there observed. Nothing but the words of God uttered by His Prophets are there chanted. And furthermore it is prescribed that no salary is attached to the services of any spiritual teacher.

And included among the nine buildings surrounding the central One is a Hotel, or Hospice, for the entertainment of travelers. Here visitors are welcomed, cared for gratis temporarily, and served in any way their need dictates. Two of these Houses of Worship are already in existence: one in 'Ishqábád, Russia, completed some years ago, the other (the central building only) in Wilmette, Illinois, a suburb of Chicago.*

---

* The House of Worship in 'Ishqábád was seized by the Soviet government in 1928, and after being damaged by an earthquake, was demolished in 1963. In addition to the House of Worship in Wilmette, IL, there are currently six other Houses of Worship in the following locations: Kampala, Uganda; Sydney, Australia; Frankfurt, Germany; Panama City, Panama; Apia, Western Samoa; New Delhi, India. Plans are currently underway for the construction of an eighth House of Worship in Santiago, Chile.

In this group of buildings we see typified for the first time in human history what Jesus described as the summing up of all the laws and all the Prophetic teachings—the love of God expressed in love for man. Is it any wonder that He described the fulfillment of His prophetic words as "The Kingdom of God on Earth!"

The Administrative Order, which ever since 'Abdu'l-Bahá's ascension has evolved and is taking shape under our very eyes in no fewer than forty countries of the world, may be considered as the framework of the Will ['Abdu'l-Bahá's Will] itself, the inviolable stronghold wherein this new-born child is being nurtured and developed. This Administrative Order, as it expands and consolidates itself, will no doubt manifest the potentialities and reveal the full implications of this momentous Document— this most remarkable expression of the Will of One of the most remarkable Figures of the Dispensation of Bahá'u'lláh. It will, as its component parts, its organic institutions, begin to function with efficiency and vigor, assert its claim and demonstrate its capacity to be regarded not only as the nucleus but the very pattern of the New World Order destined to embrace in the fullness of time the whole of mankind.[77]

So firm and mighty is this Covenant that from the beginning of time until the present day no religious dispensation hath produced its like.[78]

CHAPTER THIRTEEN

SOME DIVINE CHARACTERISTICS.
THE HUMILITY OF SERVITUDE.
THE STATION OF TRUE MANHOOD.

*The life of man is . . . divine, eternal, not mortal and
sensual. . . . The sublimity of man is his attainment
of the knowledge of God. . . . The happiness of man is
in the fragrance of the love of God. This is the highest
pinnacle of attainment in the human world.*

—'Abdu'l-Bahá,
The Promulgation of Universal Peace, p. 258

During the last three days before 'Abdu'l-Bahá left this country, I
haunted His presence. Those early December days brought a chill
to my heart as well as to my body. Although, even then, I had not
arrived at the point where I could say from my heart that I accepted
the fundamental Bahá'í teachings relative to the divine station of
Bahá'u'lláh and His place in the long line of prophetic Revelators, yet
there could be no doubt in my mind of the station of 'Abdu'l-Bahá.

What mattered if the station I ascribed was not in terms exactly
parallel to those used by the friends around Him. It sufficed me that
I saw in Him the perfect man, and that I would gladly have sacrificed
all that I had, or ever could have, to approach that perfectness.

It was not simply that He had never failed me in a response to the circumstances and conditions of daily life, which left nothing to be desired from the standpoint of wisdom, humility, courage, gentleness, and courtesy. If that were all, it would mean that I was assuming to my own judgment an expert dogmatism. Who was I to determine whether He were wise or not? Could I, in my ignorance, know anything about it? Could I judge, to any appreciable degree, His station except to compare Him with myself and any others I had ever known? From that viewpoint there could be no doubt. Incomparably was He superior. He stood out from mankind as a Mont Blanc upon a plain.

But there was something else, which those who have carefully read this chronicle must have marked, but which elusively evades descriptive words. Yet must one try, for it is this very elusive something, which does much to explain His power.

One of these fascinating and provocative characteristics was His ready laughter when alluding to subjects usually approached with extreme gravity. For instance: On the last day in New York I had my final personal interview with Him. I was saying good-bye and my heart was sad. Haltingly, I expressed this sorrow that He was leaving the country and that, in all probability, I should never see Him again. We were standing. It was actually the last good-bye. 'Abdu'l-Bahá laid His arm across my shoulders and walked with me to the door, saying that I should be with Him in all the worlds of God. And then He laughed—a hearty, ringing laugh—and I, my eyes blinded with tears. "Why does He laugh?" I thought. Nevertheless, these words, and even more, the tone in which they were uttered, and His joyous laughter, have been an illuminating light upon my path through all these years.

Another characteristic always apparent was His silence. In the world of social and intellectual intercourse to which I was accustomed, silence was almost unforgivable. From the collegiate with his, or her, "line," to the lawyer, doctor, minister, statesman—a ready answer, a witty *bon mot,* a wise remark, a knowing smile was stock-in-trade. They all had their "line," and it was upon their readiness or unreadiness to meet every occasion verbally that their reputation largely rested.

How differently 'Abdu'l-Bahá met the questioner, the conversationalist, the occasion: To the questioner He responded first with silence—an outward silence. His encouragement always was that the other should speak and He listen. There was never that eager tenseness, that restlessness so often met showing most plainly that the listener has the pat answer ready the moment he should have a chance to utter it.

I have heard certain people described as "good listeners," but never had I imagined such a "listener" as 'Abdu'l-Bahá. It was more than a sympathetic absorption of what the ear received. It was as though the two individualities became one; as if He so closely identified Himself with the one speaking that a merging of spirits occurred, which made a verbal response almost unnecessary, superfluous. As I write, the words of Bahá'u'lláh recur to me: "When the sincere servant calls to Me in prayer I become the very ear with which He heareth My reply."[79]

That was just it! 'Abdu'l-Bahá seemed to listen with my ears.

You see what I mean by saying that I am trying to describe the indescribable. All this may sound to the reader as quite fantastic. Others may not have received this impression in their contacts with Him, but this invariable characteristic of 'Abdu'l-Bahá is one of my most vivid remembrances and has been the subject of much meditation.

And when, under His encouraging sympathy, the interviewer became emptied of his words, there followed a brief interval of silence. There was no instant and complete outpouring of explanation and advice. He sometimes closed His eyes a moment as if He sought guidance from above Himself; sometimes sat and searched the questioner's soul with a loving, comprehending smile that melted the heart.

And when He finally spoke, and that modulated, resonant voice of music came, the words were so unexpected, often, so seemingly foreign to the subject, that the questioner was at first somewhat bewildered, but always, with me at least, this was followed by a calmness, an understanding, which went much deeper than the mind.

Still another characteristic from the many that crowd the memory—His penetrating insight into the very heart of every subject under discussion. Sometimes this was shown by a story in which wit and wisdom were so inextricably mingled that one was often at a loss to know whether he should laugh or weep or stand in awe.

When He was at Lake Mohonk, where He spoke to the members of the International Peace Conference, 'Abdu'l-Bahá was walking with a group of the friends one morning when they came upon a party of young people.

After a few words of greeting He said that He would tell them an oriental story: Once the rats and mice held an important conference, the subject of which was how to make peace with the cat. After a long and heated discussion it was decided that the best thing to do would be to tie a bell around the neck of the cat so that the rats and mice would be warned of his movements and have time to get out of his way.

This seemed an excellent plan until the question arose as to who should undertake the dangerous job of belling the cat. None of the rats liked the idea and the mice thought they were altogether too weak. So the conference broke up in confusion.

Everyone laughed, 'Abdu'l-Bahá with them. After a short pause He added that that is much like these Peace Conferences. Many words, but no one is likely to approach the question of who will bell the Czar of Russia, the Emperor of Germany, the President of France, and the Emperor of Japan.

Faces were now more grave. 'Abdu'l-Bahá laughed again: There is a Divine Club, He said, which shall break their power in pieces.

In the light of world events during the twenty-five years since 'Abdu'l-Bahá told that story to a youthful, happy group fresh from listening to the eloquent appeals for world peace voiced by well-meaning but impotent ones, the distractedly weak discussing how to bell the war-cat, His keen penetration into the very heart of the difficulty, and His laughing summing up of the situation in a little ancient fable, the characteristic of which I spoke, is demonstrated but only to a slight degree.

Two years later the world war broke. Some of those very youngsters who laughed with Him so lightheartedly, doubtless left their bodies in Flanders; the German warlord fled his empire, his dreams become a nightmare; the torrent flooding the world carried thrones to ruin like disintegrating dwellings in a spring freshet—the Divine Club, indeed!

On one of these final days, while waiting for the friends to gather, I was talking with one of the Persian friends, Mahmud, while the Master was busied with a small group nearby. As ever, my mind was preoccupied with watching Him. His gestures, His smile, His radiant personality were a constant fascination.

"May I ask," Mahmud was saying, "whether you speak from your pulpit about the Cause of Bahá'u'lláh at all?" "Yes," I answered, "not as often as I might wish, but I quote frequently from the writings in illustration of my subject."

"When you quote, do you mention the Author?"

"Certainly," I said, in some surprise, "I naturally give my authority."

He said, "It must require some courage, does that not arouse criticism?"

"I had not thought of the matter in that light. Why should it require courage to speak of truth without regard to its source? We are not living in the Middle Ages."

Mahmud stepped over to where 'Abdu'l-Bahá was sitting and said a few words in Persian to Him. The Master smiled over at me with that indescribably penetrating glance of which I have often spoken. He remarked that it took a *great deal of courage.*

This was on the afternoon of Dec. 3 in the Park Avenue home of a woman whose life for years had been dedicated to service in spite of the, at times, somewhat violent opposition of her influential husband, who had even gone so far as to have her examined by alienists, but who, some years later, became a devoted adherent to the cause of Bahá'u'lláh. The large drawing room was filled when the Master spoke to us. The words were few but pregnant, dealing again with those qualities which must characterize the believers.

> I offer supplication to the Kingdom of Abhá and seek extraordinary blessings and confirmations in your behalf in order that your tongues may become fluent, your hearts like clear mirrors flooded with the rays of the Sun of Truth, your thoughts expanded, your comprehension more vivid and that you may progress in the plane of human perfections.
>
> Until man acquires perfections himself, he will not be able to teach perfections to others. Unless man attains life himself, he cannot convey life to others. Unless he finds light, he cannot reflect light. We must, therefore, endeavor ourselves to attain to the perfections of the world of humanity, lay hold of everlasting life and seek the divine spirit in order that we may thereby be enabled to confer life upon others, be enabled to breathe life into others.[80]

As these words are written we recall a conversation with one of the editors of a well-known and "influential" Christian magazine. He has written and lectured much on world conditions and is an eloquent disciple of the cause of international peace. In this interview, which I had sought because of one of his books lately read, I mentioned the Bahá'í House of Worship whose impressive dome was almost within sight of where we sat. Instantly his demeanor changed.

"If you are speaking of Bahá'ísm," he said, "I have nothing more to say."

"Have you investigated its teachings?" I asked, much surprised at this strange attitude.

"No, I haven't and I have no desire to do so," he answered. And without waiting for a reply, he continued:

"That may be prejudice, and I am frank to admit that I am prejudiced."

"How can we ever attain to world peace unless we are freed from prejudice?" I said, rising to take my leave, for the interview was plainly at an end, "surely we can free ourselves from that incubus."

"Never," he said, smilingly but with great vigor, "never can we be free from prejudice: it is ineradicable in human nature."

I speak of this incident, unimportant in itself, to illustrate the unanswerable wisdom of 'Abdu'l-Bahá's words just quoted. He is not holding before us an unattainable or indefinite ideal. He is pointing out a simple and demonstrable fact. And in the light of that fact we see at once why so little real progress is made toward universal peace and unity in religion by the wordy adherents of these ideals. How plainly does prejudice, self-interest, and narrow vision underlie their words! How can the hearts clouded by such mists reflect the Sun of Truth? How can they breathe life into others when there is no sincere, self-sacrificing desire on their part to acquire life?

On the evening of the same day, 'Abdu'l-Bahá spoke briefly again to a group of Bahá'í friends of the subject, which, on these last days seemed very close to His heart and lips—the station to which those who had accepted the teachings of Bahá'u'lláh were called and expected to attain by the very fact that they had accepted them.

I remember, in this connection, a story told me by one of the friends present at a meeting of the executive committee of the New York Spiritual Assembly. 'Abdu'l-Bahá had been asked to be present. After listening to their deliberations for a half-hour or so, He calmly arose to leave.

At the door He paused a moment and surveyed the faces turned toward Him. After a moment of silence He said that He had been told that this was a meeting of the executive committee. "Yes, Master," said the Chairman.

"Then why do you not execute."

Always was His emphasis upon deeds, and deeds of such quality and purity as seemed, to those who listened, unattainable. Nevertheless there was no lowering of the standard. And He set the example. There was no doubt of that. Like the true leader, He never called upon His followers to go where He had not blazed the path.

> I have proclaimed unto you the glad tidings of the Kingdom of God and explained the wishes of the Blessed Perfection. I have set forth that which is conducive to human progress and shown you the humility of servitude.[81]

I have selected these latter words for emphasis because they indicate what seems to me to be the very heart of 'Abdu'l-Bahá's teachings.

First: His invariable example. Second: His "humility of servitude." This spirit of servitude was His distinguishing characteristic. The very title given Him by Bahá'u'lláh, 'Abdu'l-Bahá, and by which He wished always to be known and addressed, "The Servant of Glory," was indicative of the essential nature of this quality as it related to the Bahá'í teaching. He was once asked to act as honorary chairman of the National Spiritual Assembly. "'Abdu'l-Bahá is a servant," He responded simply.

> I am 'Abdu'l-Bahá and no more. I am not pleased with whosoever praises me by any other title. I am the servant of the Blessed Perfection, and I hope that this Servitude of mine will

become acceptable. Whosoever mentions any other name save this will not please me at all. 'Abdu'l-Bahá and no more. No person must praise me except by this name: "'Abdu'l-Bahá."[82]

And again:

The mystery of mysteries of these words, texts and lines, is servitude to the Holy Presence of the Beauty of 'Abhá, and effacement, evanescence and perfect dispersion before the Blessed Threshold. This is my brilliant diadem and my glorious crown. With this I will be glorified in the heavenly kingdom and the kingdom of this world. And with it I will approach unto the Beauty among the nearest ones to God, and no one is allowed to interpret other than this.[83]

'Abdu'l-Bahá says that the "conditions of existence are limited to servitude, Prophethood and Deity."[84] That is to say: Since man is incapable of attainment, either to the station of the Divine Essence or of Prophethood (except in those unique instances of the anointed Ones, which occur, roughly speaking about every thousand years), the only possible station to which he may aspire is that of servitude.

In spite of the fact that Jesus proclaimed much the same truth, this is practically an entirely new conception, originating with the teaching of Bahá'u'lláh and exemplified in every deed and word of His majestic Son.

It is important, then, that this word and its implications be examined. What does 'Abdu'l-Bahá mean by *servitude?* What possible ground can He have for asserting, as He does by implication, that unless man in this day attains that station he forfeits the right to be called man at all?

When Jesus said: "He that would be greatest among you let him be the servant of all;" "The meek shall inherit the earth." And when He washed His disciple's feet—what did He mean? What was He trying to convey? Exactly what 'Abdu'l-Bahá meant when He made the statements I have quoted above. And it is very simple and demonstrable truth.

Bahá'u'lláh says:

> Lofty is the station of man! Not long ago this exalted Word streamed forth from the treasury of Our Pen of Glory: Great and blessed is this Day—the Day in which all that lay latent in man hath been and will be made manifest. Lofty is the station of man, were he to hold fast to righteousness and truth and to remain firm and steadfast in the Cause. In the eyes of the All-Merciful a true man appeareth even as a firmament; its sun and moon are his sight and hearing, and his shining and resplendent character its stars. His is the loftiest station, and his influence educateth the world of being.[85]

Now, as though a wide window opened to a breeze from the world of explanation and understanding, 'Abdu'l-Bahá's glorification of the station of *servitude* becomes clear, or at least clearer than was possible without this new, yet eternally old, definition of man. For *servitude,* to 'Abdu'l-Bahá, was—is—the path, the only possible path to that greatness. And this, I believe, is just the greatness to which Jesus referred, the greatness of true manhood. One of the distinguishing marks of the revelation of Bahá'u'lláh is His practical explanation of Jesus' words and the inclusion of their obedience in His theophany.

"The humility of servitude" to 'Abdu'l-Bahá was His "Brilliant diadem and glorious crown." Why? Certainly not because He wished to be honored and glorified above others. That would be far from humility. No! Only because He thus, and thus only, could show others the path to greatness.

Speaking broadly, there are three possible basic relations between men: strife, cooperation, and service. Whether these relations are demonstrated in the fields of home life, commerce, education, government, or anywhere else, these three motivating impulses may be seen. Usually all three of them are present, each striving for supremacy, though often quite unconsciously. Sometimes only one or two are active.

Take the average home-life for example. There we find, let us say, a father, a mother, three or four children, and a housemaid. There is strife always to be found, even in the most idealistic home. Not an outward strife always, though differences do often arise, but always an inner commotion due to the necessary effort toward unity. Then, of course there is cooperation for this is the basis of any family life, without which it would disintegrate rapidly. Finally we see service typified by the housemaid, but active in every member in varying degrees.

Let us imagine that rare article: a perfect maidservant, a purely hypothetical character, admittedly, but admirable for the purpose of illustration.* She is efficient, cooks the most delectable dishes; she is good natured, always cheerful and happy; she is obedient, never asserts herself, never contradicts; she is wise with a homely common sense, which penetrates to the heart of a problem, whether it relates to the "master's" fondness for coffee of a certain strength, the "mistress'" liking for breakfast in bed combined with an early engagement at a committee meeting, or little Johnnie's embarrassment over a raid on the pantry resulting in tummy-agony, which must be hidden from mother. This wisdom may even be so far embracing that it involves a study of the current news and market reports so that father and mother unconsciously talk things over with her when a club paper is to be prepared or a large purchase made.

---

* It should be noted that one of the core tenets of the Bahá'í Faith is the equality of women and men, and that the author's references to "the average home-life" and a "perfect maid servant" reflect the background, culture, and prevalent attitudes of the author and the society of his time, and do not necessarily accurately represent a Bahá'í perspective.

I have sometimes amused myself with picturing the daily life of such a family. Is there any question which one of its members would be the ruling power? Which the greatest, the most indispensable one of its members? Can one not imagine the consternation in that household if "Bridget" or "Mary" should announce a severing of connection?

Take another illustration: A corner grocery, which has for its motto—*and lives up to it every instant*—"Service First." Service before profit; service before clockwatching; service before any personal consideration whatever. After all, preposterous as such an hypothetical grocery store may be, that is just what a food store should be. Does not the comfort of, even in isolated cases perhaps, the very life of the community it serves depend upon it? If the desire for profit overbalances, the result is debased and unhealthy food. The law has stringent penalties for such infraction, but such laws would be unnecessary if the spirit of true service ruled. But our imaginary, our utterly preposterous ideal store *is* ruled by that spirit. No self-sacrifice is too great for its owner and employees to ensure that perfect service is rendered, with its only objective the health, happiness, and welfare of its community.

Can one not easily picture the inevitable result? That store would be the ruler of that community. Its fame would spread over the land; its business would prosper beyond any imaginings; its owner and managers might be consulted by statesmen. It would be great. But let us allow our imaginations further rioting. Let us suppose that in addition to this spirit of service, the proprietor was possessed of a wisdom and love based upon the Sermon on the Mount. The mere suggestion of such a possibility is sufficient. Such a man would come to be possessed of a power rivaling and surpassing that of a king.

If the reader is not by this time so bored by this fantastic picture that he throws the book down in disgust, let him in imagination apply this principle to the field of education, in which teachers, students, principals, et al., are motivated by a like spirit; to the field of general commerce, of government, of international relations. Would not the happiness, prosperity, efficiency, and general welfare of the race be immeasurably advanced?

But the important thing to observe is that this picture involves the appearance on this planet of a type of man quite new in world experience. But let it be also noted that while such a man is new in actual experience, he is not new in the picturings of such men as Confucius, Buddha, Zoroaster, Moses, Jesus, and Muhammad. Such men have always held these ideals before mankind. But in the teachings of Bahá'u'lláh, and in the life and example of 'Abdu'l-Bahá, these ideals are for the first time brought to the forefront and made the basis of a New World Order.

Man is called today to the attainment of that station to which he was destined from the "Beginning which has no beginning." In the very Words of Bahá'u'lláh: "Say: We have created all that are in heaven and on earth in the nature made by God. Whosoever turneth unto this blessed Countenance shall manifest the potentialities of that inborn nature, and whosoever remaineth veiled therefrom shall be deprived of this invisible and all-encompassing grace." [86]

This, then, is why 'Abdu'l-Bahá so exalted the station of servitude. This is why He intimated that man accepting any station lower than this, any putting of self before service to others, qualifies himself as of the animal, the bestial nature, and places himself outside the pale of real manhood. It is because the definition of man is altered. That which has been hinted in the past as a possible goal is now a requisite. Man's dreams, his highest dreams, must now be realized. And the path to that realization is the path of service; its goal the attainment to the station of pure servitude.

"The sweetness of servitude is the food of my spirit." These words of the Master indicate the source of His power. His was a vastly higher quality of service than even that of my fanciful imagination in the hypothetical cases mentioned above. It went far deeper; it rose to far greater heights. It was a quality inherent in His deepest being, and manifested itself in every look, gesture, deed; I had almost said in every breath He drew. The following prayer unequivocally expresses the divine station ascribed in His heart to this quality of servitude. Can anyone reading it, with eyes from which the veil of self has fallen, fail to glimpse the glory to which manhood may rise when once the truth it hides from our blind, self-clouded eyes is clearly seen?

He is the All-Glorious!

O God, my God! Lowly and tearful, I raise my suppliant hands to Thee and cover my face in the dust of that Threshold of Thine, exalted above the knowledge of the learned, and the praise of all that glorify Thee. Graciously look upon Thy servant, humble and lowly at Thy door, with the glances of the eye of Thy mercy, and immerse him in the Ocean of Thine eternal grace.

Lord! He is a poor and lowly servant of Thine, enthralled and imploring Thee, captive in Thy hand, praying fervently to Thee, trusting in Thee, in tears before Thy face, calling to Thee and beseeching Thee, saying:

O Lord, my God! Give me Thy grace to serve Thy loved ones, strengthen me in my servitude to Thee, illumine my brow with the light of adoration in Thy court of holiness, and of prayer to Thy Kingdom of grandeur. Help me to be selfless at the heavenly entrance of Thy gate, and aid me to be detached from all things within Thy holy precincts. Lord! Give me to drink from the chalice of selflessness; with its robe clothe me, and in its ocean immerse me. Make me as dust in the pathway of Thy loved ones, and grant that I may offer up my soul for the earth ennobled by the footsteps of Thy chosen ones in Thy path, O Lord of Glory in the Highest.

With this prayer doth Thy servant call Thee, at dawntide and in the night-season. Fulfill his heart's desire, O Lord! Illumine his heart, gladden his bosom, kindle his light, that he may serve Thy Cause and Thy servants.

Thou art the Bestower, the Pitiful, the Most Bountiful, the Gracious, the Merciful, the Compassionate.[87]

CHAPTER FOURTEEN

THE DEPARTURE.
'ABDU'L-BAHÁ'S LAST WORDS IN AMERICA.
SEVEN DISTINCTIVE CHARACTERISTICS OF THE TEACHINGS.
EVIDENCES OF THE NEW WORLD ORDER.

Every Christ came to the world of mankind. There-
fore, we must investigate the foundation of divine re-
ligion, discover its reality, reestablish it and spread its
message throughout the world so that it may become
the source of illumination and enlightenment to man-
kind, the spiritually dead become alive, the spiritually
blind receive sight and those who are inattentive to
God become awakened.

—'Abdu'l-Bahá,
The Promulgation of Universal Peace, p. 626

The morning of December 5, 1912, witnessed a remarkable scene
in one of the saloon cabins of the *S. S. Celtic* as she lay in the slip
in New York harbor, yet how few realized its significance. Here was
a great modern steamship about to leave for Naples. As I went up
the gangplank, I found myself in the midst of that indeterminate,
indescribable rushing about; the bustling confusion of a depart-
ing liner. Friends saying a last good-bye; laughter with wet eyes;

petty-officers bellowing orders; whistles from passing ferryboats; uniforms, business suits, rumbling baggage trunks, women, children—and the wintry sun bright over all.

I caught sight of several of my friends and joined them on their way to the large saloon cabin, which seemed to have been given over to the farewell scene. Here the atmosphere was very different. True, the noises of the world without penetrated but were silenced by the serenity of another world. Here was 'Abdu'l-Bahá, His face a mosaic of beauty. His cream-colored robe fell to His feet. His fez slightly tipped, as I had grown accustomed to seeing it at times. In fact the position of that headdress seemed to me often indicative of His mood—humorous, slightly tipped; welcoming, a backward slant; grave and serious, firmly on His crown of silvery hair; authoritative and commanding, slightly over His dome-like brow. These may be fanciful differentiations but much of my time during my many meetings with Him had been spent in silent watchfulness of that compelling figure, and many must have noted, as had I, that one of His most characteristic movements was the involuntarily lifted hand adjusting the fez to a new angle.

My memory recalls the scene as though yesterday my eyes beheld it. The large, low-ceiled saloon was crowded. At least one hundred, possibly more of the friends were there. The Persians who had accompanied Him to this country surrounded Him—more correctly speaking, were grouped behind Him. Indicative of the Oriental attitude toward the Master was the noticeable fact that never, under any circumstances, would one of them dream of standing in front of Him, or even beside Him, unless summoned or delivering a message. When walking always were they in the rear. Even when accompanied by only one, and conversing with Him, that one always walked an appreciable few inches behind Him. When speaking with Him they rarely raised their eyes to His face. In His presence they stood as before a king. How different the Western believer's attitude! Our boasted democracy has its windy aspects under any circumstances, but when in the presence of spiritual majesty humility is freedom.

Few of us found seats. The chairs and lounges were limited and we were many. The interpreter, who had long been His secretary and was now returning with Him, stood a pace behind Him. And then He spoke. For the last time, in this world, that beloved voice resounded in my ears. I have often mentioned the quality of that voice. Never shall it be forgotten by those who truly heard it. It had a bell-like resonance unapproached by any other. It seemed to carry with it the music of another world. Almost one could imagine an accompaniment of unseen choirs.

This is my last meeting with you, for now I am on the ship ready to sail away. These are my final words of exhortation. I have repeatedly summoned you to the cause of the unity of the world of humanity, announcing that all mankind are the servants of the same God, that God is the creator of all; He is the Provider and Life-giver; all are equally beloved by Him and are His servants upon whom His mercy and compassion descend. Therefore, you must manifest the greatest kindness and love toward the nations of the world, setting aside fanaticism, abandoning religious, national and racial prejudice.

The earth is one native land, one home; and all mankind are the children of one Father. God has created them, and they are the recipients of His compassion. Therefore, if anyone offends another, he offends God. It is the wish of our heavenly Father that every heart should rejoice and be filled with happiness, that we should live together in felicity and joy. The obstacle to human happiness is racial or religious prejudice, the competitive struggle for existence and inhumanity toward each other. . . .

Beware lest ye offend any heart, lest ye speak against anyone in his absence, lest ye estrange yourselves from the servants of God. You must consider all His servants as your own family and relations. Direct your whole effort toward the happiness of those who are despondent, bestow food upon the hungry, clothe the needy, and glorify the humble. Be a helper to every helpless one, and manifest kindness to your fellow creatures in order that ye may attain the good pleasure of God. This is conducive to the illumination of the world of humanity and eternal felicity for yourselves. I seek from God everlasting glory in your behalf; therefore, this is my prayer and exhortation.[88]

After a reference to the war then being carried on in the Balkans, and the arresting sentence; in the light of what occurred two years later: "A world-enkindling fire is astir in the Balkans," He continued:—

As to you: Your efforts must be lofty. Exert yourselves with heart and soul so that, perchance, through your efforts the light of universal peace may shine and this darkness of estrangement and enmity may be dispelled from amongst men, that all men may become as one family and consort together in love and kindness, that the East may assist the West and the West give help to the East, for all are the inhabitants of one planet, the people of one original native land and the flocks of one Shepherd.

Consider how the Prophets Who have been sent, the great souls who have appeared and the sages who have arisen in the world have exhorted mankind to unity and love. This has been the essence of their mission and teaching. This has been the goal of their guidance and message. The Prophets, saints, seers and philosophers have sacrificed their lives in order to establish these principles and teachings amongst men. Consider the heedlessness of the world, for notwithstanding the efforts and sufferings of the Prophets of God, the nations and peoples are still engaged in hostility and fighting. Notwithstanding the heavenly commandments to love one another, they are still shedding each other's blood. How heedless and ignorant are the people of the world! How gross the darkness which envelops them! Although they are the children of a compassionate God, they continue to live and act in opposition to His will and good pleasure. God is loving and kind to all men, and yet they show the utmost enmity and hatred toward each other. God is the Giver of life to them, and yet they constantly seek to destroy life. God blesses and protects their homes; they rage, sack and destroy each other's homes. Consider their ignorance and heedlessness!

Your duty is of another kind, for you are informed of the mysteries of God. Your eyes are illumined; your ears are quickened with hearing. You must, therefore, look toward each other and then toward mankind with the utmost love and kindness. You have no excuse to bring before God if you fail to live according to His command, for you are informed of that which constitutes the good pleasure of God. You have heard His commandments and precepts. You must, therefore, be kind to all men; you must even treat your enemies as your friends. You must consider your evil-wishers as your well-wishers. Those who are not agreeable toward you must be regarded as those who are congenial and pleasant so that, perchance, this darkness of disagreement and conflict may disappear from amongst men and the light of the divine may shine forth, so that the Orient may be illumined and the Occident filled with fragrance, nay, so that the East and West may embrace each other in love and deal with one another in sympathy and affection. Until man reaches this high station, the world of humanity shall not find rest, and eternal felicity shall not be attained. But if man lives up to these divine commandments, this world of earth shall be transformed into the world of heaven, and this material sphere shall be converted into a paradise of glory. It is my hope that you may become successful in this high calling so that like brilliant lamps you may cast light upon the world of humanity and quicken and stir the body of existence like unto a spirit of life. This is eternal glory. This is everlasting felicity. This is immortal life. This is heavenly attainment. This is being created in the image and likeness of God. And unto this I call you, praying to God to strengthen and bless you.[89]

Such ideas and ideals have been expressed by all the noble ones of the past and present but at this great crisis in the history of mankind their implications are entirely different.

(1) They are not only exhortations; they are commands. Note the recurrence of the word "must."

(2) They are characterized by their completeness (I here refer to the full and exhaustive revelations of Bahá'u'lláh and their practical exemplification by 'Abdu'l-Bahá) and their definite application to the needs of the hour.

(3) Never in the history of mankind has the mind of the average man been so matured and prepared to listen to, and to act upon them, nor so generally aware of the pressing, immediate need of their application.

(4) For at least 1300 years such ideals and commands have not found utterance through human lips by One Who not only spoke them but lived them.

(5) These commands are addressed not to a select group, not to one nation or race, but to all peoples and individuals throughout the world, and the call is to form an entirely new world order, a new type of international civilization founded upon these divine revelations—for such is the unequivocal claim—this world order having been explicitly outlined, and directions given for its practical working, in the voluminous writings and detailed explanations of Bahá'u'lláh and 'Abdu'l-Bahá.

In order that the reader may have before him a picture of what this New World Order envisages, I quote a few words from "The Goal of the New World Order" written by Shoghi Effendi, the

Guardian of the Bahá'í Faith, in 1931. He quotes from Bahá'u'lláh's Tablet to Queen Victoria, written about 1866, as follows:

> O kings of the earth! We see you increasing every year your expenditures, and laying the burden thereof on your subjects. This, verily, is wholly and grossly unjust. Fear the sighs and tears of this wronged One, and lay not excessive burdens on your peoples. . . .
>
> Be reconciled among yourselves, that ye may need no more armaments save in a measure to safeguard your territories and dominions. . . .
>
> Be united, O kings of the earth, for thereby will the tempest of discord be stilled amongst you, and your peoples find rest, if ye be of them that comprehend. Should any one among you take up arms against another, rise ye all against him, for this is naught but manifest justice.[90]

And Shoghi Effendi comments as follows:

> What else could these weighty words signify if they did not point to the inevitable curtailment of unfettered national sovereignty as an indispensable preliminary to the formation of the future Commonwealth of all the nations of the world? Some form of a world super-state must needs be evolved, in whose favor all the nations of the world will have willingly ceded every claim to make war, certain rights to impose taxation and all rights to maintain armaments, except for purposes of maintaining internal order within their respective dominions. Such a state will have to include within its orbit an international executive adequate to enforce supreme and unchallengeable authority on every recalcitrant member of the commonwealth; a world parliament whose members shall be elected by the people in their respective countries and whose election shall be confirmed by their respective governments; and a supreme tribunal whose

judgment will have a binding effect even in such cases where the parties concerned did not voluntarily agree to submit their case to its consideration. A world community in which all economic barriers will have been permanently demolished and the interdependence of Capital and Labor definitely recognized; in which the clamor of religious fanaticism and strife will have been forever stilled; in which the flame of racial animosity will have been finally extinguished; in which a single code of international law—the product of the considered judgment of the world's federated representatives—shall have as its sanction the instant and coercive intervention of the combined forces of the federated units; and finally a world community in which the fury of a capricious and militant nationalism will have been transmuted into an abiding consciousness of world citizenship—such indeed, appears, in its broadest outline, the Order anticipated by Bahá'u'lláh, an Order that shall come to be regarded as the fairest fruit of a slowly maturing age.[91]

(6) During the ninety-three years since the message was announced by the Báb, and in the seventy-four years since the public announcement of His mission and station by Bahá'u'lláh, and—more noticeably—during the sixteen years since the establishment of the function of Guardianship and the inauguration by Shoghi Effendi of the administrative framework of the New World Order, the several millions of enrolled believers in all the countries of the world have been organized into a coherent, steadfast, self-sacrificing army, which unreservedly accepts these commands as of divine origin and is prepared to obey them unquestioningly.

The attention of the thoughtful ones amongst statesmen, scientists, and laymen has been noticeably aroused by this unprecedented phenomenon. Year by year this accelerated motion is increasing. There is therefore plainly to be seen growing up in the midst of a world of unrest, confusion, and strife, a world of uncertainties and planless effort, the actual appearance of a new type of manhood; a new conception of government and citizenship; a new vision of the practical possibilities of human life upon this planet.

(7) To whatever cause it may be ascribed it is becoming increasingly apparent that many, if not all, of the teachings of Bahá'u'lláh are being accepted by the broader minds, the wiser statesmen of the world, irrespective of their knowledge of the life, or the acceptance of the station of their Originator.

The reader may desire, and is entitled to, a proof of the last assertion. Any complete quotations from men universally accepted as more or less qualified to speak intelligently of world affairs would require a large volume. The quotations given are only meant to be indicative of a trend of modern thought which any wide reading will substantiate.

> "Cooperation must be the leading thought. Not one country only but the world must be organized into one commonwealth. National armaments must disappear and only a sufficient police force remain to keep order. Those countries in which women are most active in public affairs are democratic and peace-loving."
>
> Arthur Henderson, President of the Disarmament Conference
> at a dinner given by the Women's Organizations
> of the Consultative Group.

Here, two of the commands of Bahá'u'lláh are supported. Almost the exact wording of Bahá'u'lláh's command is used regarding the method to be followed in disarming. Also Bahá'u'lláh's words regarding the station of women in this day are acknowledged as wise.

> "The liberal scientific research—man's eternal search for truth in its vast, ever-changing forms—cannot be too highly encouraged and praised."
>
> Crown Prince Gustaf Adolf of Sweden.
> From his address at the Spring Festival, Uppsala University.

This may seem a commonplace to the reader, but when it is remembered that when Bahá'u'lláh first voiced the command that the "Independent investigation of Truth" is the first requisite in a divine civilization, such an idea was generally unacceptable. When I was a boy an energetic controversy waged for some years over whether Darwin's theory of the Origin of Species could possibly be accepted since it seemed to contradict the story of man's origin as given in Genesis. And I seem to remember that even today a certain state in this enlightened country of ours still has a statute quite rigidly enforced, which is based not upon whether the theory of evolution has an element of truth, but upon whether it can be justified by a prejudiced and ignorant interpretation of words written some thousands of years ago. Galileo, Roger Bacon, Copernicus lived not so long ago and we still have with us the Index Expurgatorius.

It is an unquestioned fact that prior to the middle of the nineteenth century, the final decision as to what constituted *truth* was almost exclusively in the hands of ecclesiastics, and the pursuit of science untrammeled was difficult, to say the least. Not until Bahá'u'lláh issued His commands relative to the oneness of science and religion did the freedom of the mind attain its birth—coincidence if you like, but there it is.

The present time is not an economic revolution but a spiritual revolution. We, the people of today, are passing through the most momentous and far-reaching changes that have taken place since the beginning of recorded history. Science has made us the undisputed masters of all the forces of Nature. There is enough grain to feed everybody. There is enough wool to clothe everybody. There is enough stone and mortar to house everybody. And yet the picture all around us is one of vast hopelessness and despair.

Something therefore must be wrong with the picture! That is what we say. Would it not perhaps be a little fairer to confess:

"Something is wrong with ourselves?"

"To have or to be!" I shall submit that terrific sentence to all who have eyes to see and ears to hear and that true spiritual courage that is the basis of all permanent progress.

Hendricks Van Loon. "To Have or to Be."

It may be that, without freedom from one's self, all other freedom is vain. . . . Perhaps in the deeper realization of our inevitable brotherhood, perhaps in our increased awareness of values other than material, there may be the germs of a lasting faith by means of which the diverse peoples of this nation may be united in a common purpose. . . . We need a unifying faith by means of which some part of the responsibilities that we are now carrying may be lifted from us, in the light of which our way may be made clearer before us.

Margaret Cary Madeira. *Atlantic Monthly.*

No system of human relationships can succeed if operated in the attitude and with the intention of mutual exploitation.

Any system will succeed if operated in the spirit of mutual service; indeed, in this spirit the need of systems would disappear.

Jas. H. Cousins. *The Young Builder.*

In all these spheres—the economic, the racial, the international, which in many places overlap—there are signs that the golden age is dawning. It will not come automatically. It will come, as reforms have always come, because some heroic souls count not their lives dear in order that they may translate from the ideal to the actual those truths by which Jesus Christ lived and for which He died.

D. G. W. Stafford, of University Temple, Seattle, at the Institute of World Affairs.

Not only in relation to our physical needs but in relation also to our mental needs does our new interrelated civilization play a vital part. Spiritually we cannot go back to the water-tight divisions, to the narrow loyalties, to the little sectarianisms which characterized the old way of life.

A new and wider trail has been blazed; and while there will undoubtedly be an occasional loss of direction, as there is at the present moment, the trend toward a world economy and a planetary consciousness is too definitely under way to be permanently reversed.

Raymond B. Fosdick. *Scientific American.*

It would be possible to continue such quotations almost indefinitely, and to cap each one with the definite command of Bahá'u'lláh; but surely any unprejudiced mind, after even a cursory study of the writings of Bahá'u'lláh and 'Abdu'l-Bahá, will find innumerable examples of the fulfillment of their commands in the daily press, current magazines, the announcements from laboratories, national council chambers, the work rooms of inventor and mechanic; "Whether we look or whether we listen" we see and hear on every hand the fulfillment of Their words, the obedience to Their commands.

While 'Abdu'l-Bahá was in this country He said to one who mourned the conditions prevailing throughout the world, then in far less distress than now, that we should not be disturbed, that whatever may occur in the future we must know always that nothing happens that does not forward the Kingdom of Bahá'u'lláh. His Will is supreme.

Speaking in Montclair, NJ, June 23, 1912, 'Abdu'l-Bahá said:

None of the Prophets of God were famous men, but They were unique in spiritual power. Love is the eternal sovereignty. Love is the divine power. By it all the kings of earth are overthrown and conquered. What evidence of this could be greater than the accomplishment of Bahá'u'lláh? He appeared in the East and was exiled. He was sent to the prison of 'Akká in Palestine. Two powerful despotic kings arose against Him. During His exile and imprisonment He wrote Tablets of authority to the kings and rulers of the world, announcing His spiritual sovereignty, establishing the religion of God, upraising the heavenly banners of the Cause of God.[92]

Again speaking at a dinner in Washington, D.C., April 22, 1912, only ten days after His arrival in this country, He said:

Today in this meeting we have an evidence of how Bahá'u'lláh through the power of the love of God has exercised a wonderful spiritual influence throughout the world. From the remotest parts of Persia and the Orient He has caused men to come to this table to meet with the people of the West in the utmost love and affection, union and harmony. Behold how the power of Bahá'u'lláh has brought the East and West together. And 'Abdu'l-Bahá is standing, serving you. There is neither rod nor blow, whip nor sword; but the power of the love of God has accomplished this.[93]

The point I am endeavoring to make is this: that Bahá'u'lláh lays claim to a divine power which overrules men and nations; that this power is the power of the love of God; that everything that is happening in this world today is evidence of that overruling power; that investigation of the commands and foresight of Bahá'u'lláh and His Exemplar compared with the events transpiring in the world since 1853 will bear testimony to the effectiveness of that power; and finally, that there is unmistakable evidence on every hand, in every quarter of the globe, amongst every type of mind and every activity, that world opinion is moving with accelerated motion into line with a world order exactly corresponding to the plan outlined by Bahá'u'lláh, promulgated and exemplified by

'Abdu'l-Bahá, and now, at this very moment, being organized, administrated, and operated by His grandson, Shoghi Effendi, from the international center at Haifa, Palestine.

What, then, is the complete picture of the situation? It is beyond the bounds of the human mind to give this picture in its fullness, and beyond the limits of this book even to portray so much of it as is within these bounds. But enough has been pointed out to allow for a brief and graphic picture of its essential elements.

We see a small group numbering several millions of souls, scattered in all parts of the world, composed of every nation, race, and creed, without reservation accepting Bahá'u'lláh as the Supreme Lawgiver for the world organization of a new order of civilization, and ready to sacrifice all, even to life itself in His service. Balancing this, and working in complete harmony with it, we see the League of Nations gradually coming into line with these laws; we see world opinion coming to a realization that such laws are indispensable if any true civilization is to exist, and we see the framework of that new order actually growing rapidly before our very eyes under the administration of Shoghi Effendi. Let him who reads investigate with open mind and ask himself whether such a movement may with wisdom be neglected.

To return to the scene on the *S. S. Celtic:* When 'Abdu'l-Bahá had finished His brief talk He requested all present to come to Him that He might take their hands in a parting expression of His love. How impressive that scene, how filled with a significance beyond words to express, how fragrant with an atmosphere of a world far removed from the sordid world around us, may only be intimated.

We slowly passed in front of Him. To each He gave a handful of the flowers massed near Him—of which, by the way, none remained when He had finished—and to each He spoke a few words of love and encouragement. When my own turn came I again forgot all but His nearness and the overwhelming fact that never again in this world would I see Him, or hear that beloved voice. I impulsively dropped to a knee, raised His hand with mine and placed it upon my head. Never shall I forget the relaxation of that arm and hand. It made no move of itself. It was a dead weight in my clasp. But His face was illumined with transcendent light.

Here was my final, indelible impression of that supreme humility, evanescence, servitude, and love, which ever characterized His slightest act, and which never failed.

The friends gathered on the wharf looked up at the figure of their Master as the ship slowly moved into the river. 'Abdu'l-Bahá stood at the rail. His white hair and beard moved by the breeze, His erect, majestic figure outlined clearly. In His hand I noticed the rosary which was His constant companion. His lips were moving. I could easily read those lips. "Alláh'u'Abhá!" "Alláh'u'Abhá!" "God the Most Glorious!" "God the Most Glorious!"

CHAPTER FIFTEEN

BY THEIR FRUITS SHALL YE KNOW THEM.
FOUR TABLETS.

If ye obey Me you will see that which We have prom-
ised you, and I will make you the friends of My Soul
in the realm of My Greatness and the Companions
of My Perfection in the heaven of My Might forever.

—Bahá'u'lláh,
"Súriy-i-Haykal,"
The Summons of the Lord of Hosts, ¶125

It was about two or three months after 'Abdu'l-Bahá had left America that I came into the realization, a conviction that has never
since wavered for an instant, of the respective stations of the Báb,
as the "First Point" of light on the horizon of the New Day; of
Bahá'u'lláh, "The Glory of God," as the Manifestation of the lights
of the "Essence in the mirrors of names and attributes,"[94] and of
His Son, 'Abdu'l-Bahá as the Center of His Covenant, the divinely
appointed exemplar, the perfect Man, Whose mission it was to
manifest the beauty of holiness in the station of perfect servitude
to God and man—"I am the servant of the servants of God."

Strangely enough this conviction was the direct outcome of
spiritual service. It became overwhelmingly apparent that for the
first time in my ministry I was able, in a deeply transforming man-

ner, to assist souls struggling in the grasp of temptation, sorrow, perplexity of mind, and confusion with all the intricate problems of life and death.

A spiritual intuition seemed to have been born—undoubtedly derived from the sublime words upon which my spirit had been feeding for many months, and still more from the personal teachings and example of 'Abdu'l-Bahá, that gave to those words that poignancy—which attracted and melted hearts. I suppose the old terminology might have used the term: "the gift of the Holy Spirit" to describe this marvelous happening. All that I know is that it was an entirely new and very humbling experience.

The teachings and example of 'Abdu'l-Bahá colored and influenced all relations with my kind. I saw even my weak attempts to adapt the teachings I had received to the needs of individual souls result so effectually that I was filled with a sensation of mingled awe and joy so new, so overwhelming, that I was carried as if on a torrent of absolute conviction into such an atmosphere of certitude that every vestige of my former doubts and uncertainties vanished as if they had never been. A voice whispered across the ages in my deepest soul: "Men do not gather grapes of thorns, nor figs from thistles." When one sees with his own eyes, human souls awakened, hearts touched with a divine afflatus, lives deeply affected, sorrow transformed into content, inward strife and turbulence calmed, by the words taken from the prayers and explanations of these divine Ones, and applied like a soothing ointment to the wounds of the soul, to doubt the Spirit from which they emanated would have been to doubt all the prophets of the past; would have been to cast discredit on the Sermon on the Mount and on all Christian tradition. "If this is not of God," I said to myself, "then there is no foundation for faith in God. I would rather be wrong with this great Faith than seemingly right with all the doubters and cavilers in the world." From the very depths of my being there came the cry as uttered by the firm believers of old: "My Lord and my God!"

Moreover, in my own life such a new orientation occurred that all events and circumstances; all thoughts and expressions; all people and conversations acquired a new significance and a new purport. It seemed as though there gradually took shape, underlying the smallest as well as the more important events of daily life, something solid, an assurance of it all being well in spite of outward seeming, which transformed the world. "He had set my feet upon a rock and established my going."

I remember that one of the members of my family greeted me one morning, as I entered the room, with the surprised ejaculation: "Well, what's the good news?" I suppose my face and bearing was that of one who had just received the announcement of exceeding good fortune.

The meaning of the words, which I had so often quoted in the more or less perfunctory manner of the theologian, came to me with a novel and striking significance: "Behold I bring you glad tidings of great joy!" And the words of Bahá'u'lláh expressing this same source of supreme happiness: "that which is the source of delight for all mankind."[95]

But it was undoubtedly the receipt of a third Tablet from the Master that completed my subjugation. I quote it simply with the prefatory remark that all communications from 'Abdu'l-Bahá are universal and may be read by any soul and applied to himself *if he fulfills the conditions of the sincere seeker.*

O thou my heavenly son:

Thy letter was received. It was a rose-garden from which the sweet fragrances of the love of God were inhaled. It indicated that you have held a meeting with the utmost joy and fragrance.

Your aim is the diffusion of the light of guidance; the resurrection of the dead hearts, the promotion of the oneness of the world of humanity and the elucidation of Truth. Unquestionably you will become confirmed therein and assisted by the invisible powers.

I have prayed on thy behalf that thou mayest become the minister of the Temple of the Kingdom and the herald of the Lord of Hosts; that thou mayest build a monastery in heaven and lay the foundation of a convent in the Universe of the Placeless; in all thy affairs that thou mayest become inspired by the Breaths of the Holy Spirit, and that thou mayest become so illumined that the eyes of all the ministers be dazzled by thy brilliancy, and may long to attain to thy station.

Thou art always in my memory. I shall never forget the days of our meeting.

Endeavor as much as thou canst that thou mayest master the Principles of Bahá'u'lláh, promulgate them all over that continent, create love and unity between the believers, guiding the people, awakening the heedless ones and resurrecting the dead.

Convey on my behalf the utmost longing to all the friends of God.

Upon thee be the Glory of the Most Glorious.

(Signed) 'Abdu'l-Bahá Abbás.

Aside from the apparent fact that this letter was a call, a summons, a trumpet-peal from a higher realm to *advance*—to "come along *up*," the meaning, the inner significance, of some of the phrases used, eluded me completely at the time and still remain only dimly apprehended.

"Assisted by the Invisible Powers"—"Minister of the Temple of the Kingdom"—"A monastery in heaven"—and a "convent in the Universe of the Placeless"—what could such strange phrases mean?

As the years have passed and more and more thoroughly I have become impregnated with the divine utterances of Bahá'u'lláh and 'Abdu'l-Bahá, meaning has emerged, elusive yet definite, vague yet alluring beyond words in its appeal to the spirit. What if the orchestra is veiled behind its screen of divine roses—is the music less entrancing, or the certainty that there is an orchestra there less convincing because of that?

In order that the reader may inhale the perfume from those roses and, perchance, hear with the inner ear the strains from that hidden orchestra, let me quote two passages from the words of 'Abdu'l-Bahá.

On April 30, 1912, He spoke in Chicago at a meeting of the Bahá'í Temple Unity Convention. From this I quote:

> Among the institutes of the Holy Books is that of the foundation of places of worship. That is to say, an edifice or temple is to be built in order that humanity might find a place of meeting, and this is to be conducive to unity and fellowship among them. The real temple is the very Word of God; for to it all humanity must turn, and it is the center of unity for all mankind. It is the collective center, the cause of accord and communion of hearts, the sign of the solidarity of the human race, the source of eternal life. Temples are the symbols of the divine uniting force so that when the people gather there in the House of God they may recall the fact that the law has been revealed for them and that the law is to unite them. They will realize that just as this temple was founded for the unification of mankind, the law preceding and creating it came forth in the manifest Word.[96]

Again: 'Abdu'l-Bahá wrote to an American believer who had asked regarding her membership in a Christian church:

> Know thou: in the day of the Manifestation of Christ many souls became portionless and deprived because they were members of the Holy of Holies in Jerusalem. Because of that membership (standing for exclusiveness and prejudice) they became veiled from His Brilliant Beauty. Therefore turn thy face to the Church of God, which consists of divine instructions and merciful exhortations. For what similarity is there between the church of stone and cement, and the Celestial Holy of Holies? Endeavor that thou mayest enter this Church

of God. Although thou hast given oath to attend the (material) church, yet thy spirit is under the Covenant and Testament of the spiritual, divine Temple. Thou shouldest protect this. The reality of Christ is the Words of the Holy Spirit. If thou art able, take a portion thereof.[97]

Does not a new significance attend the words of John the Divine, as he attempted to portray in symbolic words the coming of the Kingdom upon earth? "And I saw no temple therein; for the Lord God Almighty is the Temple of it." "And the City had no need of the sun for the Glory of God did lighten it." (Let it be remembered that the literal translation of the title "Bahá'u'lláh" is "the Glory of God.")

To be a "minister" of the Temple of this Kingdom, then, is simply to be an adherent and promulgator of the law of unity and love laid down as compulsory upon all sincere believers in the one God; to be assisted by the "Invisible Powers" is to be surrounded by those eternal forces, which ever support the courageous warriors for truth; to build a "Monastery in Heaven" and a "Convent in the Universe of the Placeless" is to build such spiritual fortresses of detachment and severance for the souls of men that "while living upon the earth they may truly be in heaven."

To be such a minister is the prerogative of every believer in the words of God and the sincere follower of His light. What a glorious world this "mound of earth" will be when all men attain even to a glimmer of this light!

Two months later a fourth Tablet was received, which again opened Portals to Freedom into a world of increasing light and beauty.

O thou my respected son:
The letter that thou hast written with the utmost love became the cause of perfect happiness. Truly, I say, thou art striving with heart and soul, to obtain the good pleasure of God. It

is assured that this blessed intention will have great effect. The good intention is like an ignited candle whose rays are cast to all parts. Now, praise be to God, that thou hast manifested the utmost effort so that thou mayest light a candle of guidance in that region, plant a tree of the utmost freshness and delicacy in the garden of the world of humanity; call the people to the divine Kingdom; become the means of the progress of intellects and souls; gather the lost sheep under the protection of the Real Shepherd; cause the awakening of the sleepy ones; bestow health upon those who are spiritually sick; enlarge the sphere of human minds; refine the moral fiber of the people and direct the wandering birds to the rose-garden of Reality.

Rest thou assured that the Eternal Outpouring shall descend upon thee, and the Confirmations of His Holiness Bahá'u'lláh shall encircle thee.

Convey to all the believers the wonderful 'Abhá greetings.

Upon thee be the Glory of the Most Glorious.

(Signed) 'Abdu'l-Bahá Abbás

Mt. Carmel,

Haifa, Syria,

March 31, 1914

Again a Call! Again a summons to dwell and work in a higher world!

There are three of these commands—for as such I have always understood and accepted them—which particularly impressed me at the time, and which ever since have been a subconscious influence upon my meditations and activities. They are these: "Become the means of the progress of intellects and souls." "Enlarge the sphere of human minds." "Refine the moral fiber of the people."

It needs but the most cursory observation of average humanity to realize the static nature of its mind, its cumbrousness, its inability to move out of its chosen or enforced rut. The mental and spiritual "sphere" in which most of us function is a very narrow one.

Our horizon is limited by our personal interests. True, the student and philosopher go beyond this and pigeonhole their knowledge and pride themselves upon their "liberality" of view, but when it comes to *action* their horizon also is limited by personal considerations. I do not forget the saints and heroes of all time who have placed truth above self, family, and life. But neither do I forget that the portion of such has ever been the stake, the dungeon, and the Cross. And, alas, it would seem that neither do "the simple, whom they call savants"[98] (as Bahá'u'lláh so trenchantly observes) forget it either. They follow truth just so far as "her ways are ways of pleasantness and all her paths are peace," but hesitate when the finger of scorn points or possessions are threatened, or family deserts.

Far be it from me to criticize or cavil at this fundamental quality of a nature common to us all. I simply point out this incontrovertible fact and that this attitude, according to the dictum of all the great and holy ones of the ages, is due to ignorance—ignorance of the true nature of life, ignorance of its infinite horizons, ignorance of its origins in the unimaginably distant past as well as of its equally unimaginable glorious future in "all the worlds of God."

It is this to which 'Abdu'l-Bahá refers when He calls one to "Become the means of the progress of intellects and souls," and "to enlarge the sphere of human minds."

As to His summons to "refine the moral fiber of the people," surely none may doubt the average flaccidity of that fiber. Our estimates of any moral issue are almost invariably decided by its personal reaction. If we test our sense of justice, for instance, by Bahá'u'lláh's definition: "Wert thou to observe justice choose for others that which thou choosest for thyself,"[99] how many of us would measure up? From the automobile driver in an accident whose first instinct is to blame the other party, to the judge on the bench whose decisions are apt to be colored by its political results, all are tarred by the same brush. And again the reason is to be found in the limited sphere of the mind. Those who do so are simply shortsighted. Their horizon is too narrow, too limited by immediate considerations, to see clearly the inevitable results. It is these results that have plainly been written on the pages of all history, the cumulative effects of which have now thrown the world into disastrous confusion and misery.

Surely if ever there were a greater need than this, that the moral fiber of the people be refined to a point where it shall be cleansed from those elements foreign to man's higher and divine nature, and He "stand forth pure and unsullied by the dross of selfishness," it would be difficult to find.

The most impressive of the Tablets received from 'Abdu'l-Bahá came to me just about the time of the outbreak of the World War, early in August of 1914. It is as follows:

> O thou respected personage:
>
> Thy letter was received. Its perusal imparted to me great hopefulness, for from its contents it became manifest that through the effects of thy entrance into the Divine Kingdom thou art progressing day by day.
>
> When this progress shall become perpetual and continual, then thou shall find the Most Great Center in the Universe of God, and shall clearly behold the Confirmations of the Holy Spirit. Thou shalt be baptized in the Fountain of Life and shalt be freed from all the laws of the world of nature.
>
> Thou shalt become illumined, merciful, heavenly—a radiant candle in the world of humanity.
>
> Endeavor as much as possible to liberate thyself wholly from human susceptibilities—so that the powers of the Kingdom may gain control over thy heart and thy spirit—to such a degree that although thou art living on the face of the earth, yet thou mayest truly be in heaven; that although outwardly thou art composed of material elements, yet spiritually thou mayest become composed of heavenly elements.

This is the everlasting glory of man! This is the eternal sub-limity in the world of existence! This is the never-ending Life! This is the Spirit incarnated in the heart of humanity!

Upon thee be the Glory of the Most Glorious.

(Signed) 'Abdu'l-Bahá Abbás
Home of 'Abdu'l-Bahá, Haifa, Syria, July 16, 1914.

It seems impossible to imagine a higher mandate, a more pro-vocative appeal, a more stimulating and suggestive contrast to or-dinary ideals or modes of thought. There is a galvanic quality to such phrases as "Find the Most Great Center in the Universe of God," "Be freed from all the laws of the world of nature," and "Liberate thyself wholly from human susceptibilities." And what shall be said regarding the hope emphatically proffered that un-der certain conditions it is possible that the "Powers of the King-dom," those higher laws and their active exponents of a celestial world, may so "gain control" of one's being that he may actually become composed of different and holy elements, and may walk this world outwardly its denizen but inwardly guided and moti-vated by influences and powers emanating from a far higher and more real world.

It is possible that the reader may consider such ideas as fantas-tic. Nor should that be an incomprehensible attitude unless he has some knowledge of the lives and teachings of Bahá'u'lláh and His Son, and—I may emphatically add—the lives and martyrdoms of thousands of their followers and lovers.

As for myself: I have seen with my own eyes a life so far above the sort of life lived by the ordinary man that any comparison based on its activation by ordinary motives is incredible. 'Abdu'l-Bahá certainly revolved around a "Center" vastly different from the ego-centeredness of mankind. He, while outwardly clothed in man's habiliments, inwardly was palpably clothed with the "characteris-tics of God." So plainly was He free from "all the laws of the world of nature" and liberated from captivity to "human susceptibilities" that one could not be in the same room with Him and not feel the atmosphere of a higher, calmer, nobler world radiating from Him.

What, then, shall be our reaction when He calls us to join Him in that world of the spirit? One of only three attitudes seems to be possible: (a) He was a visionary, an impractical idealist and not to be taken seriously. (b) He was unique in type and capabilities and spoke and acted from a background of wisdom and capacity unattainable by other men. (c) He was a Herald of a world of reality of which this phenomenal world is like an upside-down reflection; a Summoner to all men to leave the seeming and live on the plane of the *real;* an Exemplar to humanity that such an utter alteration of orientation is not only possible but imperative if any measure of happiness, tranquility, wisdom, and prosperity is to be attained.

Let us examine each of these possibilities, for there are no others and we *must* decide on one of them, unless we are willing to dodge the issue entirely and refuse to think.

(a) 'Abdu'l-Bahá's whole life contradicted this assumption that He was a visionary, an impractical idealist. When He addressed the student-body at Leland Stanford University He was introduced by its president, David Starr Jordan, in these words: "'Abdu'l-Bahá will surely unite the East and the West for *He treads the mystical 'way with practical feet.'*" He was a successful businessman and was often consulted by other men, not believers, by the way, as to the conduct of their businesses. One of His outstanding characteristics was a calm judgment in all material affairs; a poise in dealing with men and occasions of all kinds unrivaled by the most astute of captains of industry. He has been known to go into the kitchen and prepare a meal for His guests. He never failed in such small attentions as seeing that the room where His visitors were entertained contained every possible comfort, though He paid no attention to His own comfort.

In short, the slightest investigation into the facts will force the conclusion that our first hypothesis is untenable.

(b) That He was possessed of powers more than human and therefore we could not be expected to be like Him. This is the easy explanation. It is the "alibi" so often used by those who demand an excuse for the discrepancy between their ideals and actions. The modern term for this kind of thing is "rationalizing."

The difficulty of accepting it is that by its acceptance we automatically reject the teachings and example of all the great souls of the past and present. To those bred in the Christian tradition it means the placing of the Christ in the category of an unapproachable perfection and pay no regard to His constant reiteration of the necessity for "walking in His way," "loving one another as I have loved you," "taking up one's cross daily and following Me." It is also to disregard the philosophies of the noblest of mankind who make no claims to divine authority—such men as Socrates, Epictetus, Marcus Aurelius, Emerson, and countless others whose lives have proven the possibility of approximating deeds to words.

And worst of all results from such a decision, or so it seems to the writer at least, is the degrading corollary that man's progress has ceased; that the present condition of the world, which is due to man's disregard of, and unbelief in, any such world as 'Abdu'l-Bahá intimates in the above Tablet, is the normal and unchangeable condition. It means that the "laws of the world of nature" are irrevocable; that it is man's proper state for him "to be red in tooth and claw with ravin"; that there is no destiny beyond the grave and consequently no higher world of activity for which to prepare.

No! To me this is an unthinkable, a monstrous conclusion.

Let us examine without prejudice the third hypothesis, namely, that Bahá'u'lláh came into the world as the latest of the long line of Revelators of the divine will for the express purpose of opening to men the world of reality; to focus the attention of men upon a type of life, a sphere of activity that heretofore has remained more or less in the background of men's effective energies, and that His Son, 'Abdu'l-Bahá, is the living proof of man's ability to live and move and work in that world of reality and thus build in actuality that Kingdom on earth, which Jesus told us to expect and for which He commanded us to petition.

To this writer such a hypothesis is not only satisfying but supremely rational and understandable. That there is such a sphere of action (which is what is meant by the term "world") is abundantly demonstrated not only by the peaks of humanity but in varying degrees by every human soul. Man's selfishness ("that strange disease," as 'Abdu'l-Bahá designates it) has heretofore clouded that world, but within the last half-century more and more its light has shone. Our Red Cross society, our international peace organizations, The League of Nations, even our community chests, are demonstrating its existence and influential power.

Bahá'u'lláh has simply called all men to make that sphere of action the realm in which they shall *constantly* and *consciously* move, speak, and act. In effect he says to us: "You have tried it in a small degree, why not extend it to embrace every detail of life?"

In order that this may be accomplished, is it not plain that guidance is necessary? This complex world is very sick. It is dying from lack of a skilled physician. Its disease is so complicated, so affecting every part and organ, and the attending physicians—the statesmen, moralists, and idealists—so ignorant of the underlying causes, that imminent dissolution is impending. Shall we come to the despairing conclusion that there is no wise Physician? Shall we supinely acquiesce that this dissolution is assured, and stand with watch in hand at the bedside of the dying patient awaiting the inevitable hour? Or shall we, possibly as a last desperate resort, if our faithless should so wish to call it, turn to One Who at least lays claim to ability to diagnose and prescribe—One Who declares over and over again in words of matchless power and eloquence His divine power to heal? From many such I quote:

That which the Lord hath ordained as the sovereign remedy and mightiest instrument for the healing of all the world is the union of all its peoples in one universal Cause, one common Faith. This can in no wise be achieved except through the power of a skilled, an all-powerful and inspired Physician. This, verily, is the truth, and all else naught but error.[100]

And 'Abdu'l-Bahá says:

The body of the human world is sick. Its remedy and healing will be the oneness of the kingdom of humanity. Its life is the Most Great Peace. Its illumination and quickening is love. Its happiness is the attainment of spiritual perfections. It is my wish and hope that in the bounties and favors of the Blessed Perfection (one of the titles of Bahá'u'lláh) we may find a new life, acquire a new power and attain to a wonderful and supreme source of energy so that the Most Great Peace of divine intention shall be established upon the foundations of the unity of the world of men with God.[101]

And not only does Bahá'u'lláh claim the ability to diagnose and heal, but also the supreme authority to command, to lead, to conquer.

O kings of the earth! The Most Great Law hath been revealed in this Spot, this scene of transcendent splendor. Every hidden thing hath been brought to light, by virtue of the Will of the Supreme Ordainer, He Who hath ushered in the Last Hour, through Whom the Moon hath been cleft, and every irrevocable decree expounded.

Ye are but vassals, O kings of the earth! He Who is the King of Kings hath appeared, arrayed in His most wondrous glory, and is summoning you unto Himself, the Help in Peril, the Self-Subsisting.[102]

Never in all the history of the Prophets of the past have such tremendous affirmations been made, such divine authority been claimed, such power demonstrated. And let us not forget that for forty years this sublime One bore the persecutions and tortures of cruel kings and priests; that He lived to see thousands of His devoted believers suffer the same fate, even unto death; that throughout all of this long period never did He cease proclaiming His divine mission with an inflexible determination and an unconquerable majesty, which humbled in the end even His worst enemies. Let those who have shed one drop of blood in upholding their ideal of truth be the first doubters!

To those who see "with the eye of God," who possess that spiritual vision without which we are as "those who having eyes see not," is revealed that world of reality, whose "Most Great Center" is the Manifestation of God in this great Day of His Revelation.

We have been revolving around such limited centers, such petty interests, that our horizons have been circumscribed to such an extent that it is all but impossible for us to conceive a "Most Great Center" attaining to which we view the "Universe of God" spread before our wondering eyes, and scan a "Supreme Horizon" including all the sons of men; in the light of which, the Glory of which, all problems are solved, all flames of strife extinguished in that unity and love which is the basis of the laws of the universe.

Nevertheless, the Christs of the ages, the guides and leaders of mankind, have ever insisted on the reality, the supremacy of this divine world. Let such as are men of courage and action obey and follow them!

In September of 1916, when the World War was at its height, and communication between the Orient and Occident was difficult, I received a postal-card from the secretary of 'Abdu'l-Bahá, containing His final Tablet to me. It was not signed by Him and the original has not yet come to my hand, so I transcribe the postal-card as I received it so that the record may be complete.

Haifa, Syria
June 22, 1916

My dear brother in the Cause of humanity:

The reports of your services, your travels and lectures are
most stimulating to the friends in the Holy Land and conducive to the happiness of the heart of 'Abdu'l-Bahá. He loves
you and prays for your spiritual success and prosperity. He has
revealed a wonderful Tablet in your name, the translation of
which is the following:

O thou speaker in the Temple of the Kingdom!
Praise be to God that most of the time thou art traveling, going from city to city raising the melody of the Kingdom in meetings and churches, and announcing the glad-tidings of Heaven.
It is recorded in the Gospel that John the Baptist was crying
in the wilderness: "Prepare ye the way of the Lord, make His
Paths straight, for the Kingdom of God is at hand."
He was crying in the wilderness, but thou art crying in
populous cities. Although the ministers have brilliant crowns
on their heads, yet it is my hope that thou mayest crown thy
head with the diadem of the Kingdom—such a diadem whose
brilliant jewels may illuminate the dark passages of future centuries and cycles.
God says in His great Book, Qur'án, "He especializes with
His Mercy whomsoever He willeth." That is, God distinguisheth
with His favor and bestowal a number of souls and marks them
with His own seal of approval. A similar statement is revealed in
the Gospel: "Many are called but few are chosen." Now, praise
be to God that thou art one of those "few."
Appreciate thou the value of this bounty, and occupy thy time
as much as thou canst in the diffusion of the fragrances of God."
Upon thee be greetings and praise.
(Signed) 'Abdu'l-Bahá Abbás.

CHAPTER SIXTEEN

CONCLUSION

*The holy Manifestations of God come into the world
to dispel the darkness of the animal, or physical, nature of man, to purify him from his imperfections in
order that his heavenly and spiritual nature may
become quickened, his divine qualities awakened, his
perfections visible, his potential powers revealed and
all the virtues of the world of humanity latent within
him may come to life.*

—'Abdu'l-Bahá,
The Promulgation of Universal Peace, pp. 656–57

So here is the story. Not what it should be as an attempt toward the
portrayal of what, to me, has seemed the perfect life, but so far as
the influence which that life has had upon my own, it has been un-
reserved. For eight months that Figure moved before me. In spite
of the twenty-five years that have elapsed, still is it distinct and vital. Memory has pictures, which words may never paint. However
sadly incomplete and inadequate the endeavor to portray that life
may be, it has been a great happiness to make the attempt. I lay it
before the reader with sincere humility and love.

How could such a picture be complete? The brief span of years,
which we dare to speak of as "life," is so confused with details for-

eign to the true issues involved that when there enters upon this scene One Who lives with calm assurance in a world in which confusion is unknown, yet Who understands the turmoil of men's hearts and knows the remedy, how could it be possible for one still in that anarchy of thought and action adequately to portray Him Who brings illumination? How draw the picture graphically? How make others see and hear as He did?

To me there is only one way in which that life may even feebly be understood. An assumption must be made and a clear-cut conviction arrived at. This may be simply stated. It is this:

The world of phenomena, the "contingent world," the world as ordinarily accepted, is not the *real* world. The life we live from day to day with its monotonous round of eating and drinking; its sleeping and waking hours; its routine of work, play, study, birth, and death; its varieties of poverty and wealth, of learned and ignorant, of powerful and weak—all this is a mask hiding the face of reality. The endless attempts to solve the riddle clothed in high-sounding titles—philosophy, education, science, statesmanship—are all a species of groping in the dark.

Life does not "begin at forty," it begins in God. We do not "live on twenty-four hours a day"; "In Him we live and move and have our being," and ages of preparation precede this little "life," and ages to come are its fulfillment.

Scholasticism provides no answer to the demands of men for a satisfaction of those primal needs of the spirit. Religion, as generally understood—being, as it is, a mixture of tradition, social convention, and more or less correct estimates of the immediate problems confronting the people, and all savored with a salt that has lost its savor—provides no satisfaction to the hungry souls of men. In all this confusion of thought and action, no rock is found upon which man may plant his spiritual feet and be confident in his treading.

If this is not the real world, where is it? What is it? How find it? As I have intimated, the answer is plain enough to those who are not *entirely* "submerged in the sea of materialism." Most of mankind may be likened to a man lost in a London fog so that the well-known way to his own door is blotted out. The fog, which blinds our spiritual vision, is composed of the "selfish disorders, intellectual maladies, spiritual sicknesses, imperfections and vices,"[103] which surround us and hold us in thralldom. The Prophets of God, the will and love of God enshrined in the temple of man, have brought the light of the Sun of Reality, which alone can dissipate the fog, place man upon the right path, and free him from that thralldom.

The Eternal Christ coming to the aid of distracted humanity about once in every thousand years alone is the Portal to Freedom. Ever to the keen of vision, the quick of hearing, the possessors of heart, His divine voice calling to enter, His loving hands pointing and assisting, have been apparent.

Again, in this Day in which we live our little span of years, has the latest of these "Sign-Posts" to the path declared His Mission and issued His Call.

It was my inestimable privilege to watch and talk with, for a period of eight months, the Son of Bahá'u'lláh, the Center of His Covenant, the perfect exemplar of His word and life; the One by Whom He "shall cause them to manifest the signs of His sovereignty and might upon earth."[104]

Here I saw a man Who, outwardly, like myself, lived in the world of confusion, yet, inwardly, beyond the possibility of doubt, lived and worked in that higher and real world. All His concepts, all His motives, all His actions, derived their springs from that "World of Light." And, which is to me, a most inspiring and encouraging fact, He took it for granted that you and I, the ordinary run-of-the-mill humanity, could enter into and live and move in that world if we would.

To those who have read this chronicle with the "eye of heart," some glimmer of conviction may have come that such a world is open to them, such a life may be approximated for themselves, such a portal may be entered by their feet, such a freedom be attained. It is with this hope that my story has been told.

January 7, 1937

NOTES

1. The author here appears to be paraphrasing the words of Bahá'u'-lláh, and possibly referring to the following passage found in *Tablets of Bahá'u'lláh*, p. 199: "Whoso quickeneth a soul hath verily quickened all mankind."

2. The author here refers to an early edition of what is now known as the Book of Certitude or Kitáb-i-Íqán, one of the major works of Bahá'u'lláh, which has since been masterfully translated by Shoghi Effendi (Bahá'í Publishing, 2003). An early translation of the work was rendered by 'Ali Khuli Khán and published under the title "The Book of Assurance."

3. Bahá'u'lláh, in *Bahá'í Prayers*, p. 96.

4. It should be noted that the word "authoritative" here, in reference to a saying of 'Abdu'l-Bahá, from a Bahá'í perspective is misleading. The recorded or reported utterances of 'Abdu'l-Bahá cannot be taken to be authoritative statements of the Bahá'í teachings, nor should they be considered Bahá'í scripture.

5. The author may here be referring to an earlier translation of a passage no longer in circulation. The wording used is similar to one of the Persian Hidden Words of Bahá'u'lláh in which reference is made to the ". . . mystic chalice from the hands of the celestial Youth." See Bahá'u'-lláh, the Hidden Words, Persian, no. 70.

6. The author here appears to be referring to the wording of an early translation of the passage used as the epigraph of this chapter. See Bahá'u'lláh, *Prayers and Meditations*, p. 275. Previous editions of *Portals to Freedom* contained an early translation, which rendered the phrase "Horizon of detachment" as "Horizon of renunciation."

7. Bahá'u'lláh, "Súriy-i-Haykal," *The Summons of the Lord of Hosts*, ¶125.

8. 'Abdu'l-Bahá, *Tablets of Abdu'l-Bahá, vol. 3,* p. 515.

9. E. G. Browne, quoted in Shoghi Effendi, *God Passes By,* p. 194.

10. The author here appears to be referring to the wording of an early translation of the Seven Valleys. For the current, most up-to-date edition of this work of Bahá'u'lláh, see Bahá'u'lláh, *The Seven Valleys and the Four Valleys.* Wilmette, IL: Bahá'í Publishing Trust, 1991.

11. Ibid.

12. The author here appears to be quoting from a passage of an early translation of the Kitáb-i-Íqán, which would have been in circulation at the time of his writing. For the current, most up-to-date edition of the Kitáb-i-Íqán, or Book of Certitude, translated by Shoghi Effendi, see Bahá'u'lláh, *The Kitáb-i-Iqán.* Wilmette, IL: Bahá'í Publishing, 2003.

13. Bahá'u'lláh, *Epistle to the Son of the Wolf,* p. 141.

14. Bahá'u'lláh, *Prayers and Meditations,* p. 25; 'Abdu'l-Bahá, quoted in Universal House of Justice, *Wellspring of Guidance,* p. 126; Bahá'u'lláh, quoted in *Bahá'í Scriptures,* p. 246.

15. Bahá'u'lláh, Kitáb-i-Íqán, ¶231.

16. The author appears here to be making reference to the following words of Bahá'u'lláh from the Hidden Words, Arabic, no. 66: ". . . souls shall be perturbed as they make mention of Me. For minds cannot grasp Me nor hearts contain Me."

17. 'Abdu'l-Bahá, *The Promulgation of Universal Peace,* p. 179.

18. Ibid., pp. 179–83.

19. Ibid.

20. Ibid., p. 181.

21. Bahá'u'lláh, quoted in Shoghi Effendi, *The Promised Day is Come,* p. 30.

22. 'Abdu'l-Bahá, *The Promulgation of Universal Peace,* pp. 193–98.

23. 'Abdu'l-Bahá, in *Bahá'í Prayers,* p. 120.

24. See Bahá'u'lláh, Kitáb-i-Íqán, ¶66.

25. Bahá'u'lláh, Kitáb-i-Aqdas, ¶1, 2.

26. Bahá'u'lláh, in *Bahá'í Prayers,* p. 118.

27. Bahá'u'lláh, Kitáb-i-Aqdas, ¶65.

28. 'Abdu'l-Bahá, quoted in J. E. Esslemont, *Bahá'u'lláh and the New Era,* p. 196.

29. Bahá'u'lláh, Kitáb-i-Aqdas, ¶67.

30. See J. E. Esslemont, *Bahá'u'lláh and the New Era*, p. 195.

31. 'Abdu'l-Bahá, *Tablets of 'Abdu'l-Bahá, vol. 2*, p. 325.

32. Ibid., p. 474.

33. 'Abdu'l-Bahá, in *Bahá'í World Faith*, pp. 372–73.

34. 'Abdu'l-Bahá, *Tablets of 'Abdu'l-Bahá, vol. 2*, p. 325.

35. 'Abdu'l-Bahá, *Paris Talks*, no. 58.5–8.

36. 'Abdu'l-Bahá, *Tablets of 'Abdu'l-Bahá, vol. 3*, p. 648.

37. The Báb, quoted in Nabíl-i-A'zam, *The Dawn-Breakers*, p. 94.

38. 'Abdu'l-Bahá, *Tablets of 'Abdu'l-Bahá, vol. 1*, p. 87.

39. 'Abdu'l-Bahá, in *Bahá'í Prayers*, pp. 29–30.

40. The author here appears to be quoting an early translation of a Tablet of Bahá'u'lláh titled "Words of Wisdom." The current translation reads: "The source of all learning is the knowledge of God." See Bahá'-u'lláh, *Tablets of Bahá'u'lláh Revealed after the Kitáb-i-Aqdas*. Wilmette, IL: Bahá'í Publishing Trust, 1988 [p. 156].

41. Bahá'u'lláh, The Seven Valleys, p. 25.

42. 'Abdu'l-Bahá, *Paris Talks*, no. 22.9–10.

43. See Bahá'u'lláh, Kitáb-i-Íqán, ¶28–30.

44. See Bahá'u'lláh, *Gleanings from the Writings of Bahá'u'lláh*, no. 130.

45. The author appears here to be quoting a passage from an early translation of The Seven Valleys. For the most up-to-date and current edition of that work, see Bahá'u'lláh, *The Seven Valleys and the Four Valleys*. Wilmette, IL: Bahá'í Publishing Trust, 1991.

46. 'Abdu'l-Bahá, *The Promulgation of Universal Peace*, pp. 367–69.

47. Bahá'u'lláh, "Lawh-i-Aqdas," *Tablets of Bahá'u'lláh*, p. 7.

48. The author appears here to be quoting a passage from an early translation of The Seven Valleys. For the most up-to-date and current edition of that work, see Bahá'u'lláh, *The Seven Valleys and the Four Valleys*. Wilmette, IL: Bahá'í Publishing Trust, 1991.

49. Bahá'u'lláh, The Seven Valleys, p. 6.

50. The author appears here to be quoting a passage from an early translation of The Seven Valleys. For the most up-to-date and current edition of that work, see Bahá'u'lláh, *The Seven Valleys and the Four Valleys*. Wilmette, IL: Bahá'í Publishing Trust, 1991.

51. 'Abdu'l-Bahá, *The Promulgation of Universal Peace*, p. 608.

52. Ibid., p. 609.

53. Ibid., p. 615.

54. Ibid., pp. 630–31.

55. The author appears here to be referring to the wording of a passage from an early translation of The Seven Valleys. For the most up-to-date and current edition of that work, see Bahá'u'lláh, *The Seven Valleys and the Four Valleys*. Wilmette, IL: Bahá'í Publishing Trust, 1991.

56. 'Abdu'l-Bahá, *The Promulgation of Universal Peace,* p. 632.

57. Ibid.

58. Ibid., pp. 634–35.

59. Ibid., pp. 635–36.

60. Ibid., pp. 636–37.

61. Ibid., pp. 638–39.

62. The passage referred to here is from an early translation of the words of Bahá'u'lláh found in a volume titled *Bahá'í Scriptures* [p. 135], which is no longer in print.

63. 'Abdu'l-Bahá, *The Promulgation of Universal Peace,* pp. 400–401.

64. Ibid., p. 415.

65. Ibid., p. 528.

66. Ibid., p. 640.

67. Ibid., pp. 640–41.

68. Bahá'u'lláh, Hidden Words, Arabic, no. 2.

69. 'Abdu'l-Bahá, *The Promulgation of Universal Peace,* p. 641.

70. Ibid.

71. 'Abdu'l-Bahá, quoted in J. E. Esslemont, *Bahá'u'lláh and the New Era,* p. 163.

72. 'Abdu'l-Bahá, *The Promulgation of Universal Peace,* p. 641.

73. Ibid.

74. Ibid.

75. Ibid., p. 642.

76. Ibid.

77. Shoghi Effendi, *World Order of Bahá'u'lláh,* p. 144.

78. 'Abdu'l-Bahá, quoted in ibid., p. 146.

79. The author appears here to be referring to the wording of a passage from an early translation of The Seven Valleys. For the most up-to-date and current edition of that work, see Bahá'u'lláh, *The Seven Valleys and the Four Valleys*. Wilmette, IL: Bahá'í Publishing Trust, 1991.

80. 'Abdu'l-Bahá, *The Promulgation of Universal Peace*, p. 645.

81. Ibid., pp. 649–50.

82. 'Abdu'l-Bahá, in *Bahá'í Scriptures*, p. 284.

83. Ibid., p. 266.

84. 'Abdu'l-Bahá, *Some Answered Questions*, p. 230.

85. Bahá'u'lláh, "Kitáb-i-'Ahd," *Tablets of Bahá'u'lláh*, p. 220.

86. Bahá'u'lláh, "Súriy-i-Haykal," *Summons of the Lord of Hosts*, ¶51.

87. 'Abdu'l-Bahá, in *Bahá'í Prayers*, pp. 332–33.

88. 'Abdu'l-Bahá, *The Promulgation of Universal Peace*, pp. 660–61.

89. Ibid., pp. 662–63.

90. Bahá'u'lláh, *Summons of the Lord of Hosts*, ¶179–82.

91. Shoghi Effendi, *The World Order of Bahá'u'lláh*, pp. 40–41.

92. 'Abdu'l-Bahá, *The Promulgation of Universal Peace*, pp. 294–95.

93. Ibid., p. 59.

94. Bahá'u'lláh, The Seven Valleys, p. 5.

95. Bahá'u'lláh, "Lawḥ-i-Ḥikmat," *Tablets of Bahá'u'lláh*, p. 139.

96. 'Abdu'l-Bahá, *The Promulgation of Universal Peace*, p. 89.

97. 'Abdu'l-Bahá, in *Bahá'í World Faith*, p. 390.

98. The passage referred to here is from an early translation of the words of Bahá'u'lláh found in a volume titled *Bahá'í Scriptures* [p. 135], which is no longer in print.

99. The passage referred to here is from an early translation of the words of Bahá'u'lláh found in a volume titled *Bahá'í Scriptures* [p. 134], which is no longer in print.

100. Bahá'u'lláh, *Gleanings from the Writings of Bahá'u'lláh*, no. 120.3.

101. 'Abdu'l-Bahá, *The Promulgation of Universal Peace*, p. 26.

102. Bahá'u'lláh, *Gleanings from the Writings of Bahá'u'lláh*, no. 105.4.

103. 'Abdu'l-Bahá, *The Promulgation of Universal Peace*, p. 365; Ibid., p. 286.

104. Bahá'u'lláh, "Súriy-i-Haykal," *Summons of the Lord of Hosts*, ¶8.

BIBLIOGRAPHY

WORKS OF BAHÁ'U'LLÁH

Epistle to the Son of the Wolf. New ed. Translated by Shoghi Effendi. 1st ps
   ed. Wilmette, IL: Bahá'í Publishing Trust, 1988.
Gleanings from the Writings of Bahá'u'lláh. Translated by Shoghi Effendi.
   Wilmette, IL: Bahá'í Publishing, 2005.
The Hidden Words. Translated by Shoghi Effendi. Wilmette, IL: Bahá'í
   Publishing, 2002.
The Kitáb-i-Aqdas: The Most Holy Book. 1st ps ed. Wilmette, IL: Bahá'í
   Publishing Trust, 1993.
The Kitáb-i-Íqán: The Book of Certitude. Translated by Shoghi Effendi.
   Wilmette, IL: Bahá'í Publishing, 2003.
Prayers and Meditations by Bahá'u'lláh. Translated by Shoghi Effendi. 1st
   ps ed. Wilmette, IL: Bahá'í Publishing Trust, 1987.
The Seven Valleys and the Four Valleys. New ed. Translated by Ali-Kuli
   Khan and Marzieh Gail. Wilmette, IL: Bahá'í Publishing Trust, 1991.
The Summons of the Lord of Hosts: Tablets of Bahá'u'lláh. Wilmette, IL:
   Bahá'í Publishing, 2006.
Tablets of Bahá'u'lláh revealed after the Kitáb-i-Aqdas. Compiled by the
   Research Department of the Universal House of Justice. Translated by
   Habib Taherzadeh et al. Wilmette, IL: Bahá'í Publishing Trust, 1988.

Works of 'Abdu'l-Bahá

Paris Talks: Addresses Given by 'Abdu'l-Bahá in 1911. Wilmette, IL: Bahá'í Publishing, 2011.

Promulgation of Universal Peace: Talks Delivered by 'Abdu'l-Bahá during His Visit to the United States and Canada in 1912. Compiled by Howard MacNutt. 2nd ed. Wilmette, IL: Bahá'í Publishing Trust, 2007.

Some Answered Questions. Compiled and translated by Laura Clifford Barney. 1st pocket-size ed. Wilmette, IL: Bahá'í Publishing Trust, 1984.

Tablets of 'Abdul-Bahá Abbas. 3 vols. New York: Bahai Publishing Society, 1909–16.

Works of Shoghi Effendi

God Passes By. New ed. Wilmette, IL: Bahá'í Publishing Trust, 1974.

The Promised Day Is Come. 1st pocket-size ed. Wilmette, IL: Bahá'í Publishing Trust, 1996.

The World Order of Bahá'u'lláh: Selected Letters. 1st pocket-size ed. Wilmette, IL: Bahá'í Publishing Trust, 1991.

Compilations of Bahá'í Writings

Bahá'u'lláh, the Báb, and 'Abdu'l-Bahá. *Bahá'í Prayers: A Selection of Prayers Revealed by Bahá'u'lláh, the Báb, and 'Abdu'l-Bahá.* New ed. Wilmette, IL: Bahá'í Publishing Trust, 1991.

Bahá'u'lláh and 'Abdu'l-Bahá. *Bahá'í Scriptures: Selections from the Utterances of Bahá'u'lláh and 'Abdu'l-Bahá.* Edited by Horace Holley. 2nd ed. New York: Bahá'í Publishing Committee, 1928.

Bahá'u'lláh and 'Abdu'l-Bahá. *Bahá'í World Faith: Selected Writings of Bahá'u'lláh and 'Abdu'l-Bahá.* 2nd ed. Wilmette, IL: Bahá'í Publishing Trust, 1976.

Other Works

Esslemont, J. E. *Bahá'u'lláh and the New Era: An Introduction to the Bahá'í Faith*. Wilmette, IL: Bahá'í Publishing, 2006.

Nábil-i-A'ẓam [Muḥammad-i-Zarandí]. *The Dawn-Breakers: Nabíl's Narrative of the Early Days of the Bahá'í Revelation*. Translated and edited by Shoghi Effendi. Wilmette, IL: Bahá'í Publishing Trust, 1932.

For more information about the Bahá'í Faith,
or to contact Bahá'ís near you,
visit http://www.bahai.us/
or call
1-800-22-UNITE

Bahá'í
PUBLISHING
AND THE BAHÁ'Í FAITH

Bahá'í Publishing produces books based on the teachings of the Bahá'í Faith. Founded over 160 years ago, the Bahá'í Faith has spread to some 235 nations and territories and is now accepted by more than five million people. The word "Bahá'í" means "follower of Bahá'u'lláh." Bahá'u'lláh, the founder of the Bahá'í Faith, asserted that He is the Messenger of God for all of humanity in this day. The cornerstone of His teachings is the establishment of the spiritual unity of humankind, which will be achieved by personal transformation and the application of clearly identified spiritual principles. Bahá'ís also believe that there is but one religion and that all the Messengers of God—among them Abraham, Zoroaster, Moses, Krishna, Buddha, Jesus, and Muḥammad—have progressively revealed its nature. Together, the world's great religions are expressions of a single, unfolding divine plan. Human beings, not God's Messengers, are the source of religious divisions, prejudices, and hatreds.

The Bahá'í Faith is not a sect or denomination of another religion, nor is it a cult or a social movement. Rather, it is a globally recognized independent world religion founded on new books of scripture revealed by Bahá'u'lláh.

Bahá'í Publishing is an imprint of the National Spiritual Assembly of the Bahá'ís of the United States.

OTHER BOOKS AVAILABLE FROM
BAHÁ'Í PUBLISHING

'Abdu'l-Bahá in America
Robert H. Stockman
$18.00 U.S. / $20.00 CAN
Trade Paper
ISBN 978-1-931847-97-1

The amazing account of the journey of 'Abdu'l-Bahá across much of the United States to share the message of the oneness of humanity and the principles of universal peace.

'Abdu'l-Bahá in America is the account of the journey of 'Abdu'l-Bahá, eldest son of Bahá'u'lláh and appointed head of the Bahá'í Faith after his father's passing, across much of the United States in 1912. His exhausting yet exhilarating 239-day trek from coast to coast took him to fifty cities and towns, where he delivered up to four talks a day—about four hundred total—to approximately ninety-three thousand people about Bahá'u'lláh's message of the oneness of humanity and the principles of universal peace. This historic visit to the United States planted the seeds that would take root and germinate into the present-day American Bahá'í community.

The author has meticulously researched the journey of 'Abdu'l-Bahá by combing through discourses as well as the diary of his traveling companion, which describes almost every major event during the journey as well as many private scenes and frank comments by 'Abdu'l-Bahá. The extensive research includes the examination of newspaper and magazine articles published at the time of this historic visit, as well as hundreds of pages of unpublished telegrams, letters, diaries, and memoirs.

Spirit of Faith
THE HUMAN SOUL
Bahá'í Publishing
$12.00 U.S. / $14.00 CAN
Hardcover
ISBN 978-1-61851-000-6

A collection of uplifting prayers and writings that focuses on the human soul for spiritual seekers of all faiths.

Spirit of Faith: The Human Soul is a compilation of writings and prayers that focus on the human soul and the qualities of this remarkable and unique aspect of our existence. Spiritual seekers of all faiths will relish these uplifting passages that offer a great deal of insight into the nature and significance of the human soul—a subject that has never been so extensively explored in the religious texts of the past. This collection contains writings from Bahá'u'lláh, the Báb, and 'Abdu'l-Bahá.

The *Spirit of Faith* series explores a range of topics—such as the unity of humanity, the eternal covenant of God, the promise of world peace, and much more—by taking an in-depth look at how the writings of the Bahá'í Faith view these issues. The series is designed to encourage readers of all faiths to think about spirituality, and to take time to pray and meditate on these important topics.

Talks by 'Abdu'l-Bahá
THE EXISTENCE OF GOD
Bahá'í Publishing
$14.00 U.S. / $16.00 CAN
Hardcover
ISBN 978-1-61851-001-3

A spiritually uplifting and thought-provoking collection of talks that offers insight into the ability to know and worship God.

Talks by 'Abdu'l-Bahá: The Existence of God is a collection of talks given by 'Abdu'l-Bahá—the son and appointed successor of Bahá'u'lláh, the Prophet and Founder of the Bahá'í Faith—during his historic journey to Europe and North America in 1911 and 1912. Speaking in front of multiple audiences, 'Abdu'l-Bahá offered simple yet profound and logical proofs for the existence of God, and discussed humankind's relationship with its Creator. The talks included here present convincing and thought-provoking explanations for some of the weightiest and most complex theological questions we face when trying to untangle the mysteries of life.

The Promulgation of Universal Peace
TALKS DELIVERED BY 'ABDU'L-BAHÁ
DURING HIS VISIT TO THE UNITED STATES
AND CANADA IN 1912
'Abdu'l-Bahá
$25.00 U.S. / $27.00 CAN
Hardcover
ISBN 978-1-931847-98-8

A special centenary edition marking the 100th anniversary of the talks delivered by 'Abdu'l-Bahá during his historic journey through North America in 1912.

The Promulgation of Universal Peace is a collection of 140 talks given by 'Abdu'l-Bahá—the son and appointed successor of Bahá'u'lláh, the Prophet and Founder of the Bahá'í Faith—during his extensive tour of North America in 1912. This compilation touches on a wide range of subjects including the coming of age of the human race, the oneness and continuity of the Prophets of God, and the oneness of religion as a social force for establishing world order and peace. These talks serve as a priceless resource for studying the language and personal example of one of the most significant religious figures in recent history.